OLYMPIAD WORKBOOK

INTERNATIONAL MATHEMATICS OLYMPIAD

AF365895

- **01** Learning Objectives
- **02** Multiple Choice Questions
- **03** HOTS (Achievers Section)
- **04** Model Test Paper
- **05** Answer Keys and Solutions
- **06** OMR Answer Sheet

V&S PUBLISHERS

Published by:

V&S PUBLISHERS

F-2/16, Ansari road, Daryaganj, New Delhi-110002
☎ 23240026, 23240027 • *Fax:* 011-23240028
✉ info@vspublishers.com • 🌐 www.vspublishers.com

 **Online Brandstore: amazon.in/vspublishers**

Regional Office : Hyderabad
5-1-707/1, Brij Bhawan (Beside Central Bank of India Lane)
Bank Street, Koti, Hyderabad - 500 095
☎ 040-24737290
✉ vspublishershyd@gmail.com

Follow us on:   

BUY OUR BOOKS FROM: | AMAZON | | FLIPKART |

DISCLAIMER

PUBLISHER'S NOTE

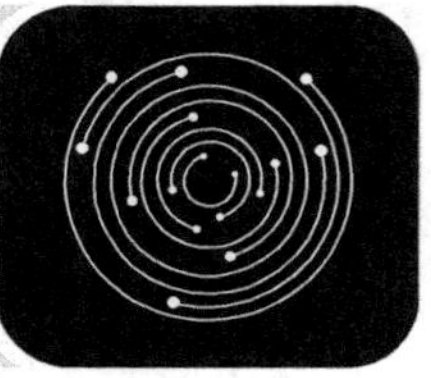

V&S Publishers has carved a significant niche in the publishing industry over the last decade, having successfully published more than 1000 titles across 9 languages spanning over 50 subject categories. Being known for the quality of content, we have built a reputation of excellence and reliability. We have consistently delivered **"Value & Substance"** to our readers, through a wide range of titles across a variety of genres covering school books, fiction and non-fiction that caters to different people from every section of the society.

The **Olympiad Guidebooks for classes 1-10** across all subjects, launched almost a decade ago, under the **GEN X Imprint**, became a go-to-source for the school students in no time, owing to their invaluable and substantive content written in a guidebook pattern,.

Having successfully sold a million copies of the same and in response to demand by both students as well as shopkeepers nationwide; we now present before you our newly launched **Olympiad Workbook Series**, designed for **classes 1-10 across 4 subjects**.

The workbooks are meticulously curated by a team of experienced educators, researchers and subject matter experts, edited by professionals and peer reviewed by teachers. The team has poured its efforts and expertise into creating a crisp and concise workbook which will help and guide the students to the path of success in Olympiad exams. The **MCQs** identified will not only help in scoring top marks in Olympiads but also inculcate a sense of deeper understanding of the subject, by way of solving **HOTS** and referring to complete solutions at the end of the book.

Here we present our new release– **OLYMPIAD WORKBOOK (IMO) CLASS–1** having following features:

- ☞ Based on the latest syllabi
- ☞ MCQs with comprehensive coverage of topics
- ☞ HOTS Questions liberally included
- ☞ A dedicated chapter on logical reasoning
- ☞ Model test paper for thorough practice
- ☞ Sample OMR sheet for real time simulation

We have made sure through our best efforts, that this workbook strictly follows the latest syllabi and patterns of the Olympiad Examination.

As **V&S Publishers** continuously strive to enhance the readability and maintain the credibility of our academic publications, we seek the support of our valuable readers in influencing and enriching the lives of future generations of students.

P.S. While every care has been taken to ensure the correctness of the content, if you come across any error, howsoever minor, do not hesitate to discuss with teachers while pointing that out to us in no uncertain terms.

We wish you all the best for your exams!

DISTINCTIVE FEATURES

01 — Learning Objectives

They list the whole chapter as subtopics, helping the teachers to guide children in a step-by-step manner.

02 — Multiple Choice Questions

MCQs act as an excellent learning aid, helping you to understand and work on your mistakes.

03 — HOTS (Achievers Section)

The High Order Thinking Questions aim to help the student to solve Application-based questions and gain practical understanding of the subject.

04 — Model Test Paper

Model test paper are provided at the end of each book, which help the student to test the knowledge which they have gained after thorough reading of all chapters.

05 — Answer Key

Detailed Answer Key along with explanations aid the pupil to indentify, understand the mistakes they make during the course of Olympiad preparation.

CONTENTS

NUMBERS

LEARNING OBJECTIVES

➤ Numerals and Counting Numbers
➤ Formation of Greatest and Smallest Numbers

➤ Number Sense (Two-Digit Numbers)
➤ Number Names (Numbers upto 100)

MULTIPLE CHOICE QUESTIONS

1. Which of the following has 6 objects?

(A) 

(B) 

(C) 

(D) 

2. Which of the following has three objects?

(A) 

(B) 

(C) 

(D) 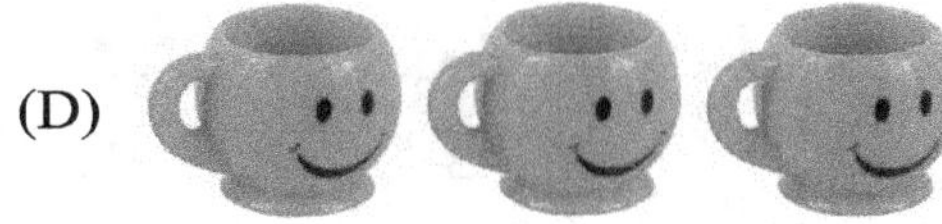

3. The greatest one- digit number is 9. What is its number name?

(A) Ten (B) Nine

(C) Five (D) Two

4. Which of the following is correct?
   (A) 7–Six
   (B) 6–Three
   (C) 5–Five
   (D) 9–Eight

5. Choose the one that is wrong.
   (A) Four – 4
   (B) Seven – 7
   (C) Nine – 9
   (D) One – 0

6. Which of the following is correct?

(A)	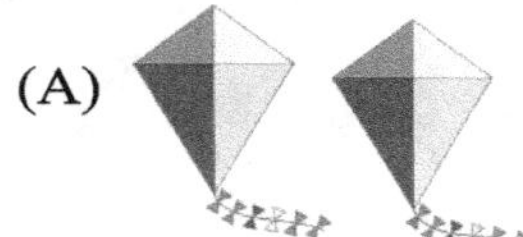	7
(B)		5
(C)		3
(D)		8

7. Choose the correct number of objects for "Four".

   (A) 

   (B) 

   (C)

   (D) 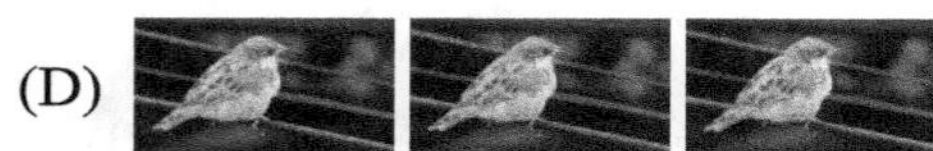

8. Which of the following is matched correctly?

(A)		2
(B)		8
(C)		9
(D)		3

9. Match the number of objects to their number names.

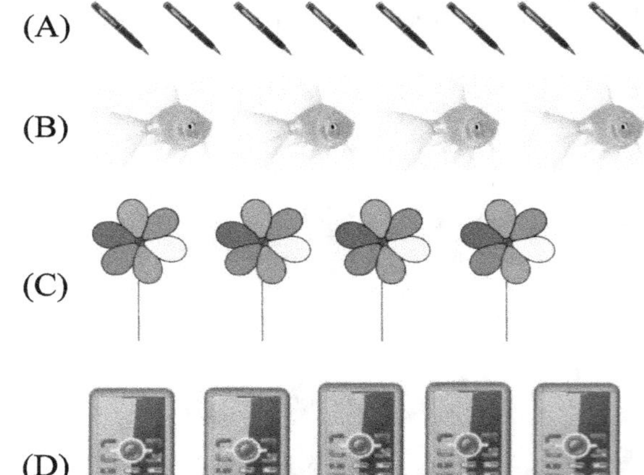

	Column I		Column II
(A)		(i)	Seven
(B)		(ii)	Three
(C)		(iii)	Four
(D)		(iv)	Five

   (A) A - i, B - ii, C - iii, D - iv
   (B) A - iv, B - ii, C - i,   D - iii
   (C) A - ii, B - iv, C - i,   D - iii
   (D) A - iii, B - ii, C - i,   D - iv

10. Select the group with 8 objects.

    (A)

    (B)

    (C)

    (D)

11. Match the numbers to the objects.

	Column I		Column II
(A)	5	(i)	
(B)	2	(ii)	
(C)	8	(iii)	
(D)	9	(iv)	

(A) A - i, B - iv, C - ii, D - iii
(B) A - iii, B - iv, C - i, D - ii
(C) A - ii, B - iii, C - iv, D - i
(D) A - iii, B - ii, C - iv, D - i

12. Choose the number name for the number of objects in the box

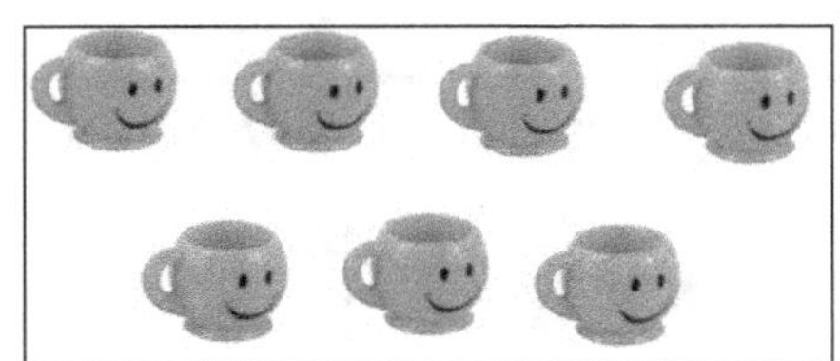

(A) Nine (B) Seven
(C) Six (D) Eight

13. Choose the correct number of objects for 'Ten'.

(A) 

(B) 

(C) 

(D) 

14. What is the ordinal number of 7?
(A) First (B) Seventh
(C) Sixth (D) Ninth

15. Which number comes after 28?
(A) Twenty nine (B) Twenty six
(C) Twenty seven (D) Twenty three

16. Which of the following is 1 more than 4?
(A) 

(B) 

(C) 

(D)  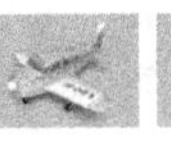 

17. Choose the correct number of the given objects.

(A) 8 (B) 10
(C) 9 (D) 7

18. Which object is at fourth position in the set given?

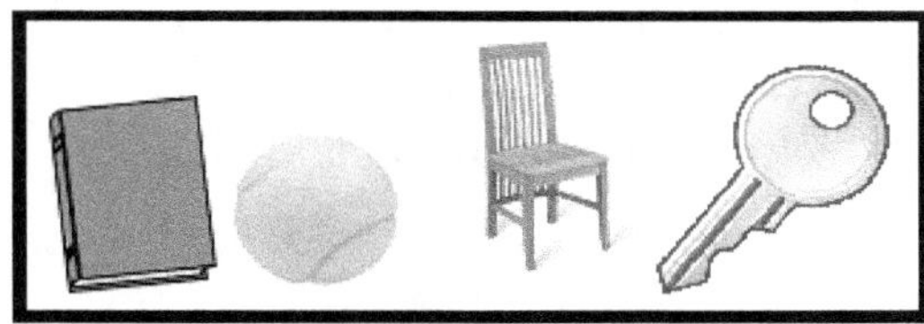

(A) Ball
(B) Chair
(C) Key
(D) Book

19. Who is standing in the third place in the line?

(A) Ashu
(B) Navneet
(C) Shraddha
(D) Ashima

20. Which bowl has minimum number of apples

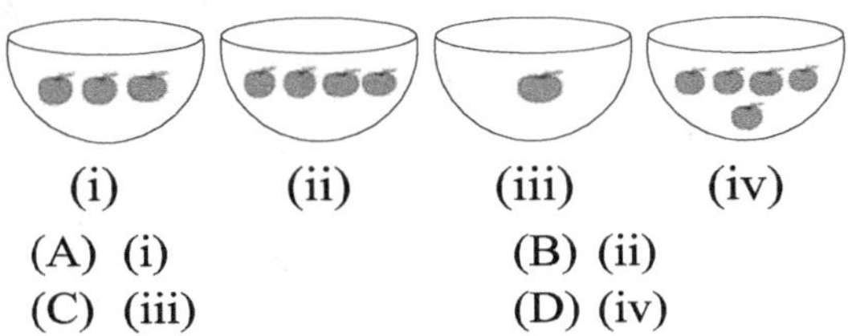

(i) (ii) (iii) (iv)

(A) (i) (B) (ii)
(C) (iii) (D) (iv)

21. What is the number name of the smallest two-digit number?

    (A) One   (B) Zero

    (C) Ten   (D) Nine

22. Which of the following has numbers in an order?

(A)	4	2	0	6
(B)	3	5	7	10
(C)	7	9	2	3
(D)	6	7	8	5

23. Which of the following has objects 1 less than 8?

    (A) 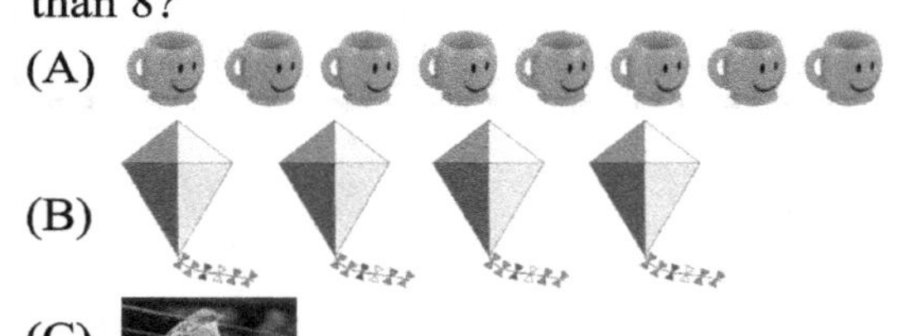

    (B) 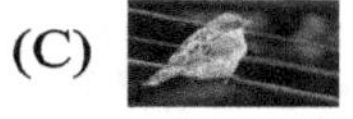

    (C)

    (D) 

24. Match the objects that are same in numbers.

Column I	Column II
(A)	(i)

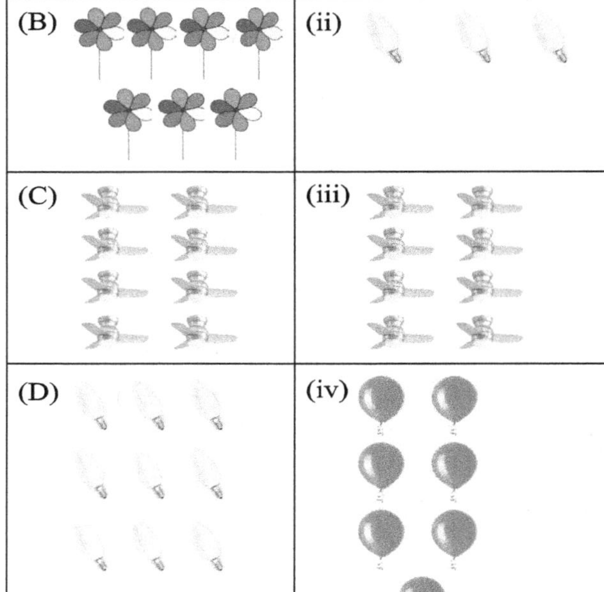

25. Choose the correct subtraction sentence for the given picture.

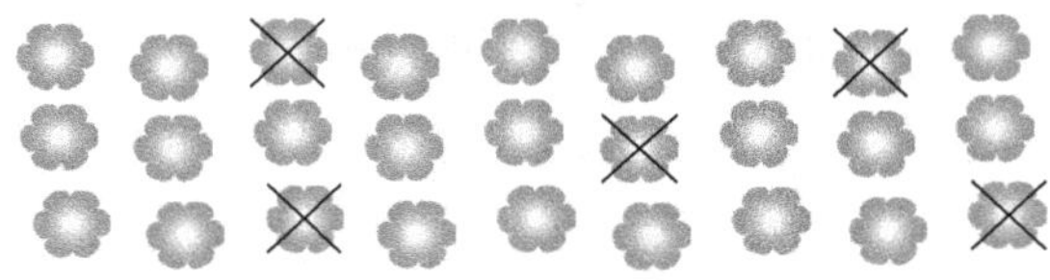

    (A) 2 tens 3 ones – 4 ones

    (B) 2 tens 4 ones – 5 ones

    (C) 2 tens 7 ones – 5 ones

    (D) 2 tens 4 ones – 4 ones

Darken Your Choice with HB Pencil

1.	Ⓐ Ⓑ Ⓒ Ⓓ	6.	Ⓐ Ⓑ Ⓒ Ⓓ	11.	Ⓐ Ⓑ Ⓒ Ⓓ	16	Ⓐ Ⓑ Ⓒ Ⓓ	21.	Ⓐ Ⓑ Ⓒ Ⓓ
2.	Ⓐ Ⓑ Ⓒ Ⓓ	7.	Ⓐ Ⓑ Ⓒ Ⓓ	12.	Ⓐ Ⓑ Ⓒ Ⓓ	17.	Ⓐ Ⓑ Ⓒ Ⓓ	22.	Ⓐ Ⓑ Ⓒ Ⓓ
3.	Ⓐ Ⓑ Ⓒ Ⓓ	8.	Ⓐ Ⓑ Ⓒ Ⓓ	13.	Ⓐ Ⓑ Ⓒ Ⓓ	18.	Ⓐ Ⓑ Ⓒ Ⓓ	23.	Ⓐ Ⓑ Ⓒ Ⓓ
4.	Ⓐ Ⓑ Ⓒ Ⓓ	9.	Ⓐ Ⓑ Ⓒ Ⓓ	14.	Ⓐ Ⓑ Ⓒ Ⓓ	19.	Ⓐ Ⓑ Ⓒ Ⓓ	24.	Ⓐ Ⓑ Ⓒ Ⓓ
5.	Ⓐ Ⓑ Ⓒ Ⓓ	10.	Ⓐ Ⓑ Ⓒ Ⓓ	15.	Ⓐ Ⓑ Ⓒ Ⓓ	20.	Ⓐ Ⓑ Ⓒ Ⓓ	25.	Ⓐ Ⓑ Ⓒ Ⓓ

ADDITION

LEARNING OBJECTIVES

- ➤ Properties of Addition
- ➤ Addition of Two-Digit Numbers (without regrouping)
- ➤ Addition of Two-Digit Numbers (with regrouping)

MULTIPLE CHOICE QUESTIONS

1. Choose the correct addition fact for the given figure

and

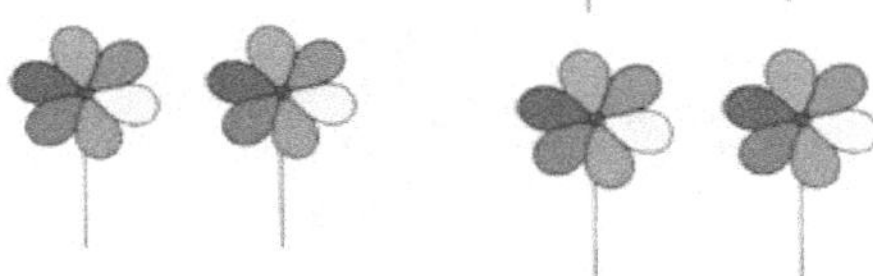

is

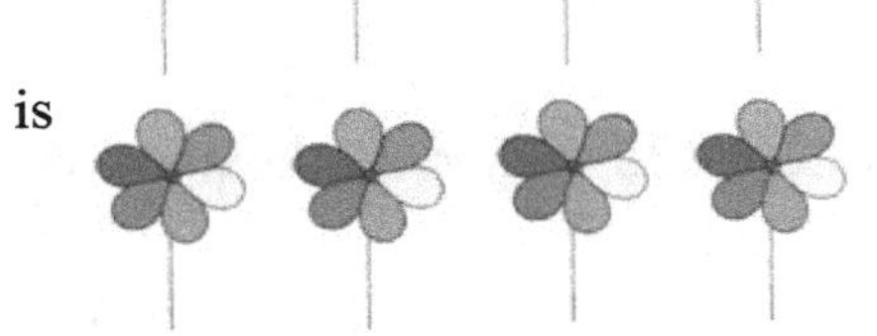

   (A) $4 + 4 = 8$ (B) $4 + 3 = 7$
   (C) $3 + 4 = 8$ (D) $3 + 3 = 8$

2. Look at the given figure.

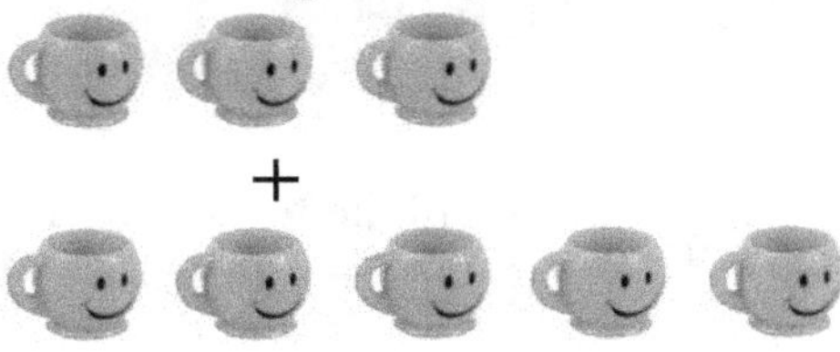

   $3 + 5 = ?$

   Find the number which comes in place of the question mark.
   (A) 9   (B) 8
   (C) 10   (D) 7

3. The adding machine adds 4 to any number that is put in it and sends the sum out. What is the sum when 5 is put into the machine?
   (A) 6   (B) 8
   (C) 3   (D) 9

4. Which of the following is incorrect sum?
   (A) $6 + 3 = 9$ (B) $6 + 4 = 11$
   (C) $5 + 4 = 9$ (D) $4 + 4 = 8$

5. Look at the figure below :

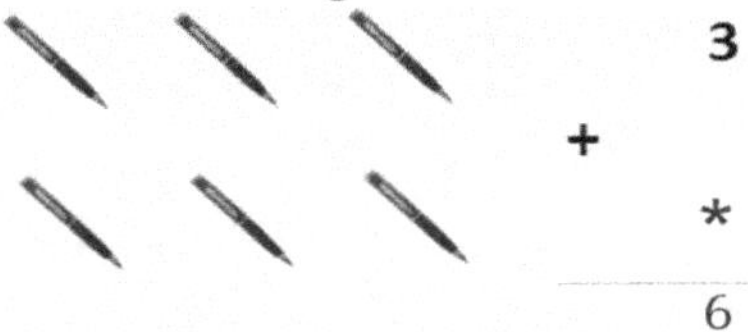

   Which number must be placed in place of '*'.
   (A) 0   (B) 3
   (C) 2   (D) 6

6. There are 7 apples in a basket. 2 more apples are put in it. How many apples are there in the basket?
   (A) 9   (B) 5
   (C) 7   (D) 0

Question 7 to 10 : Look at the figure given :

Class 1A		Class 1B		Class 1C	
21	23	24	20	21	20

7. How many students in all are there in class 1A?
   - (A) 41
   - (B) 43
   - (C) 42
   - (D) 44

8. How many girls are in class 1A, 1B and 1C altogether?
   - (A) 40
   - (B) 63
   - (C) 43
   - (D) 36

9. How many boys are in classes 1A and 1C?
   - (A) 42
   - (B) 44
   - (C) 41
   - (D) 40

10. Which two classes have the same number of girls?
   - (A) 1A and 1C
   - (B) 1A and 1B
   - (C) 1B and 1C
   - (D) Either A or B

11. Which of the following is correct sum?
   - (A) $3 + 4 = 9$
   - (B) $5 + 5 = 10$
   - (C) $2 + 6 = 9$
   - (D) $1 + 5 = 8$

12. Which is more?

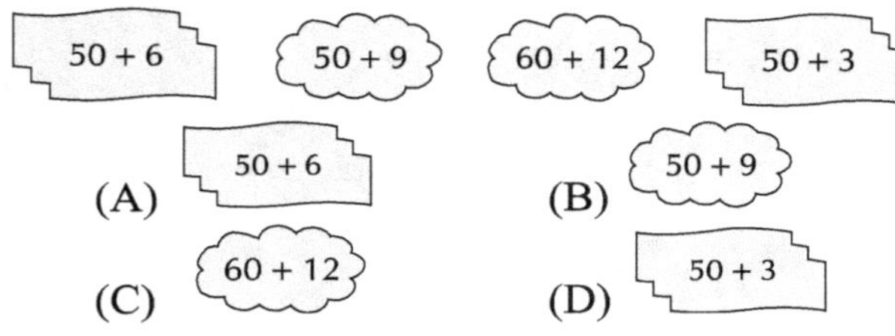

   - (A) $50 + 6$
   - (B) $50 + 9$
   - (C) $60 + 12$
   - (D) $50 + 3$

13.

20 Flowers   +   54 Flowers   = ... flowers,

   - (A) 80
   - (B) 74
   - (C) 82
   - (D) 79

14. I have 5 chocolates. Sonu gave me 4 more. Ravi gave me 3 more. How many sweets I have?
   - (A) $3 + 4 + 2 = 9$
   - (B) $5 + 4 + 3 = 12$
   - (C) $3 + 2 + 6 = 11$
   - (D) $3 + 4 + 6 = 13$

15. Number of flower in both boxes

= _______

Box A	Box B

   - (A) $8 + 5 = 13$
   - (B) $6 + 4 = 10$
   - (C) $8 + 6 = 14$
   - (D) $8 + 4 = 12$

16. Shraddha and Shubhra are playing a card game.

   What is the sum of the numbers of Shubhra's cards?
   - (A) 8
   - (B) 5
   - (C) 3
   - (D) 10

17. Golu collected 35 stamps and Ankit collected 43 stamps.

   How many stamps will the boys have in all?
   - (A) 75
   - (B) 78
   - (C) 87
   - (D) 68

OLYMPIAD WORKBOOK (IMO) CLASS – 1

18. Shraddha got 38 marks in science and 50 marks in maths.

How many marks did she get in all?

(A) 68   (B) 58

(C) 88   (D) 80

19. Radha's mother bought 10 apples on Monday, 14 apples on Wednesday and 25 apples on Sunday. How many apples did her mother buy altogether?

(A) 47   (B) 40

(C) 49   (D) 48

20. Priya has 6 dolls.

Pooja has 3 dolls.

Total number of dolls = …………

(A) 12

(B) 11

(C) 10

(D) 9

HOTS (ACHIEVERS SECTION)

21. What comes in between?

(A) 31 + 4   (B) 30 + 4

(C) 32 + 4   (D) 33 − 4

22. Add the balloons given below and choose the correct option. 

(A) 

(B)

(C) 

(D)

23. 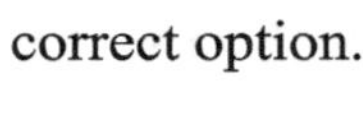

(A)   (B)

(C)   (D)

24. There are 4 legs in a chair. In a room there are 3 chairs. How many legs do these three chairs have?

(A) 7 legs   (B) 11 legs

(C) 12 legs   (D) none of these

25. In a garden there are 4 plants of Marigold, 3 plants of Jasmine and 7 plants of roses. How many plants are there in all in the garden?

(A) 14 plants   (B) 12 plants

(C) 16 plants   (D) 18 plants

Darken Your Choice with HB Pencil

1.	Ⓐ Ⓑ Ⓒ Ⓓ	6.	Ⓐ Ⓑ Ⓒ Ⓓ	11.	Ⓐ Ⓑ Ⓒ Ⓓ	16	Ⓐ Ⓑ Ⓒ Ⓓ	21.	Ⓐ Ⓑ Ⓒ Ⓓ
2.	Ⓐ Ⓑ Ⓒ Ⓓ	7.	Ⓐ Ⓑ Ⓒ Ⓓ	12.	Ⓐ Ⓑ Ⓒ Ⓓ	17.	Ⓐ Ⓑ Ⓒ Ⓓ	22.	Ⓐ Ⓑ Ⓒ Ⓓ
3.	Ⓐ Ⓑ Ⓒ Ⓓ	8.	Ⓐ Ⓑ Ⓒ Ⓓ	13.	Ⓐ Ⓑ Ⓒ Ⓓ	18.	Ⓐ Ⓑ Ⓒ Ⓓ	23.	Ⓐ Ⓑ Ⓒ Ⓓ
4.	Ⓐ Ⓑ Ⓒ Ⓓ	9.	Ⓐ Ⓑ Ⓒ Ⓓ	14.	Ⓐ Ⓑ Ⓒ Ⓓ	19.	Ⓐ Ⓑ Ⓒ Ⓓ	24.	Ⓐ Ⓑ Ⓒ Ⓓ
5.	Ⓐ Ⓑ Ⓒ Ⓓ	10.	Ⓐ Ⓑ Ⓒ Ⓓ	15.	Ⓐ Ⓑ Ⓒ Ⓓ	20.	Ⓐ Ⓑ Ⓒ Ⓓ	25.	Ⓐ Ⓑ Ⓒ Ⓓ

SUBTRACTION 

3

➤ Properties of Subtraction
➤ Subtraction of Two - Digit Numbers (without regrouping)
➤ Subtraction of Two - Digit Numbers (with regrouping)

MULTIPLE CHOICE QUESTIONS

1. What is 4 tens 3 ones minus 2 tens 2 ones?
   (A) 21 (B) 12
   (C) 23 (D) 23

2. Golu had

He gave  to his brother.

How many are left with him?

(A) 

(B) 

(C) 

(D)

3. How is 12 less than 30 written?
   (A) $30 - 12 = 18$ (B) $30 - 18 = 12$
   (C) $18 - 12 = 6$ (D) $30 - 6 = 24$

4. Which is same as $13 - 3$?
   (A) $11 - 5$ (B) $15 - 5$
   (C) $12 - 4$ (D) $9 - 3$

5. In Class I, there are 89 students. 42 of them are girls. How many boys are there in class I?
   (A) 82 (B) 42
   (C) 67 (D) 47

6. 68 oranges were in a basket. 44 were put in a bag.

How many oranges are left in the basket?
   (A) 84 (B) 24
   (C) 48 (D) 42

7. 2 tens 5 ones − 1 ten 2 ones = ?
   (A) 12 (B) 14
   (C) 13 (D) 15

8. 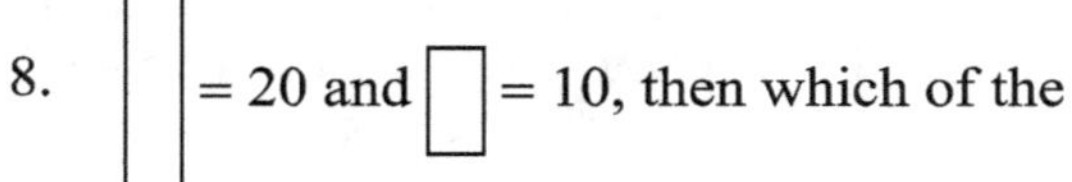 $= 20$ and $\square = 10$, then which of the following is correct?

(A) 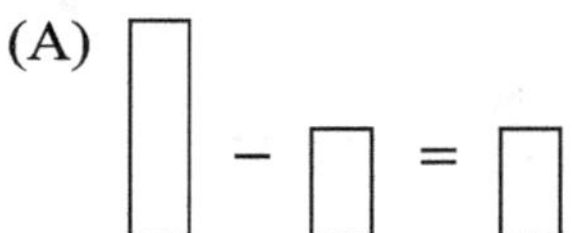

(B) 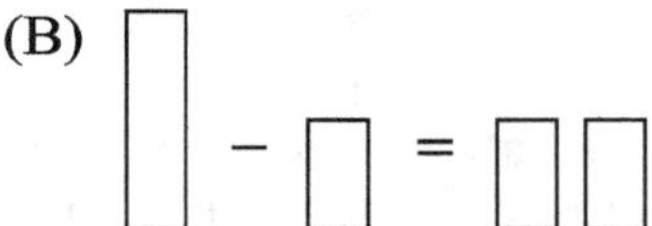

(C) 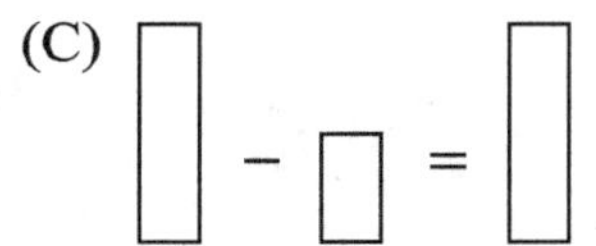

(D) 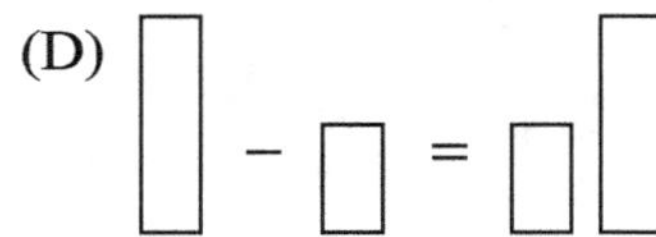

9. 

(A) 5 (B) 4
(C) 3 (D) 2

10. The difference between the greatest and the smallest number shown in the figure is __________.

(A) 64
(B) 82
(C) 81
(D) 28

98 95	
44	35
61	48
16	25

11. Which of the following is the another way of 7 less than 10?

(A) $10 - 7 = 3$ (B) $7 - 5 = 2$
(C) $12 - 5 = 7$ (D) $12 + 5 = 17$

12. 40 − 30 = ?

(A) 15 (B) 10
(C) 11 (D) 6

13. 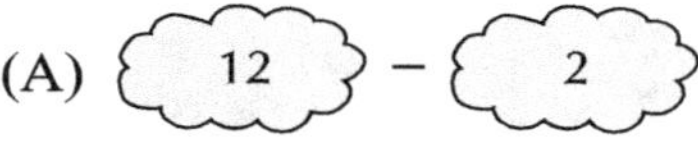

How many balloons are left?
(A) 3 (B) 4
(C) 5 (D) 7

14. There are  in a pond jumped off. How many are left?

(A) $7 - 2 = 4$ (B) $8 - 2 = 6$
(C) $7 - 2 = 3$ (D) $7 - 2 = 1$

15. Which subtraction sentence gives same value as $8 - 2$?

(A) $12 - 2$

(B) $12 - 6$

(C) $12 - 4$

(D) $15 - 5$

16. Divesh had 69 marbles. He gave 35 marbles to Kiran. How many marbles are left with Divesh?

(A) 34 (B) 45
(C) 49 (D) 36

17. A book has 55 pages. Nonu reads 40 pages. How many pages are left to be read?

(A) 20
(B) 15
(C) 25
(D) 45

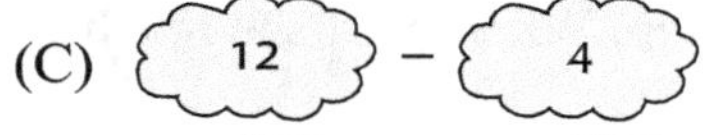

18. Shraddha has 99 sweets. She gave away 46 of them to her sister Shubhra. How many sweets does Shraddha have?

(A) 53 (B) 43
(C) 63 (D) 56

19. A shopkeeper sold 25 bags on Monday. He sold 5 bags less on Tuesday. How many bags are sold on Tuesday?
(A) $18 - 2 = 16$
(B) $25 - 5 = 20$
(C) $18 + 3 = 21$
(D) $18 - 16 = 2$

20. Manali baked 20 cakes. She gave 3 cakes to Mahima. How many cakes are left with her?
(A) 12
(B) 15
(C) 17
(D) 16

HOTS (ACHIEVERS SECTION)

21. Which of the following shows the least value?

(A) 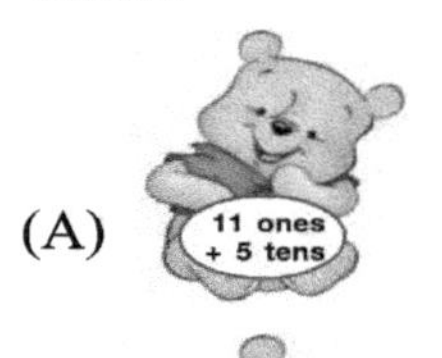

(B) 

(C) 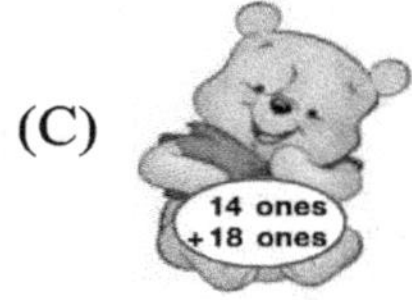

(D) 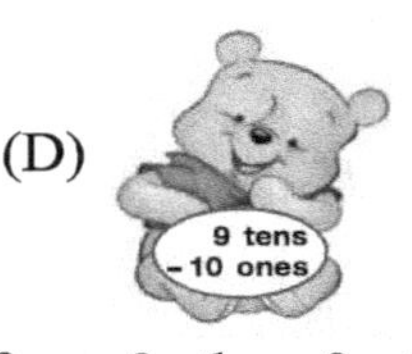

22. Garima jumps 2 steps from 0, then 3 steps and then 1 step. Where will she reach ?

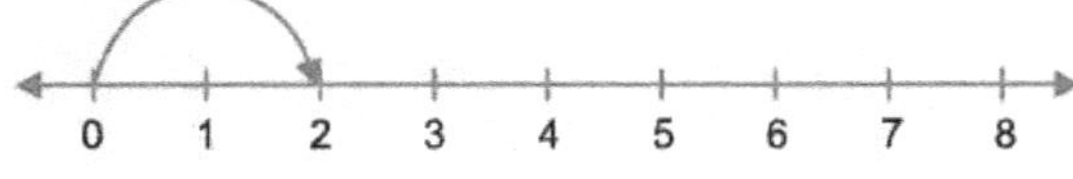

(A) 6th step
(B) 7th step
(C) 8th step
(D) 5th step

23. Tanuj drinks a few glasses of juice. There are___glasses of juice left. Tanuj drinks______glasses of juice.

(A) 4, 3
(B) 7, 5
(C) 7, 4
(D) 3, 8

24. How many more balloons do we need to add to the given set in order to have 20 balloons in total?

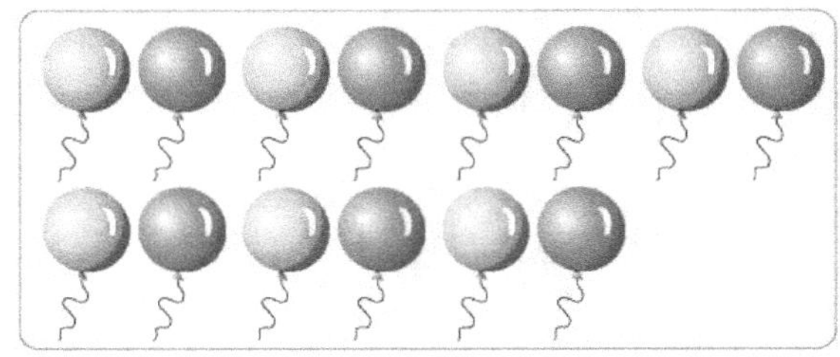

(A) 14
(B) 6
(C) 13
(D) 7

25. Which number comes in the place of R?

$R - 9 = 13$

(A) 20
(B) 22
(C) 21
(D) 24

<hr>

Darken Your Choice with HB Pencil

1.	A B C D	6.	A B C D	11.	A B C D	16	A B C D	21.	A B C D
2.	A B C D	7.	A B C D	12.	A B C D	17.	A B C D	22.	A B C D
3.	A B C D	8.	A B C D	13.	A B C D	18.	A B C D	23.	A B C D
4.	A B C D	9.	A B C D	14.	A B C D	19.	A B C D	24.	A B C D
5.	A B C D	10.	A B C D	15.	A B C D	20.	A B C D	25.	A B C D

OLYMPIAD WORKBOOK (IMO) CLASS – 1

LENGTHS, WEIGHTS & COMPARISONS

LEARNING OBJECTIVES

➤ Length ➤ Weight ➤ Capacity

MULTIPLE CHOICE QUESTIONS

1. Which of the following is shortest length?
   (A) 15 cm
   (B) 30 cm
   (C) 28 cm
   (D) 32 cm

2. Which square is the biggest?
   (A) ☐
   (B) ☐
   (C) ☐
   (D) ☐

3. Which of the following is smallest circle?
   (A) ○
   (B) ○
   (C) ○
   (D) ○

4. Which kite has the shortest tail??
   (A) 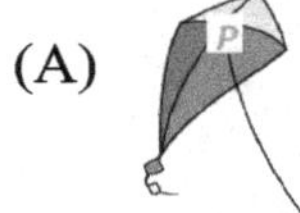
   (B) 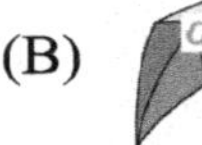
   (C) 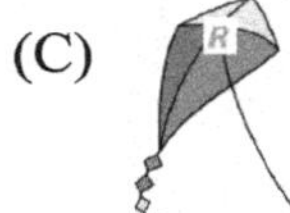
   (D) 

5. Which of the following is the lightest?
   (A) 
   (B) 
   (C) 
   (D) 

6. Which of these is lighter than  ?
   (A) 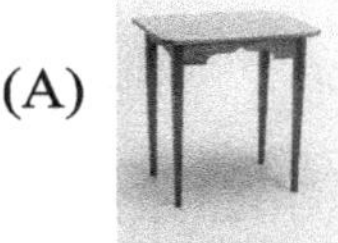
   (B) 
   (C) 
   (D) 

7. Which of the two glasses have same height?
   (A) Q and S
   (B) P and R
   (C) P and Q
   (D) R and S

8. Spider __________ is the farthest to the top of the ladder.

(A) P   (B) Q
(C) R   (D) S

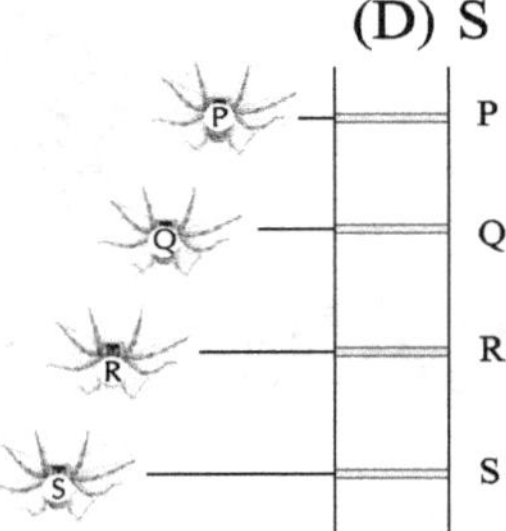

9. Which of the following picture shows the ball 1 is equal to ball 2?

(A)
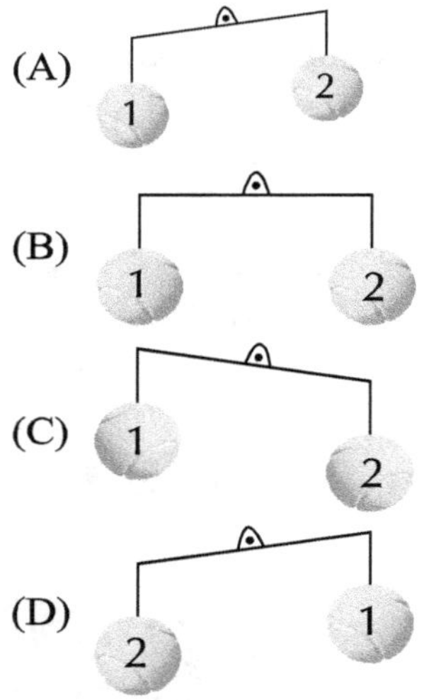

(B)

(C)

(D)

10. Which object is thinner than pencil?.

(A)

Nail

(B)

Bottle

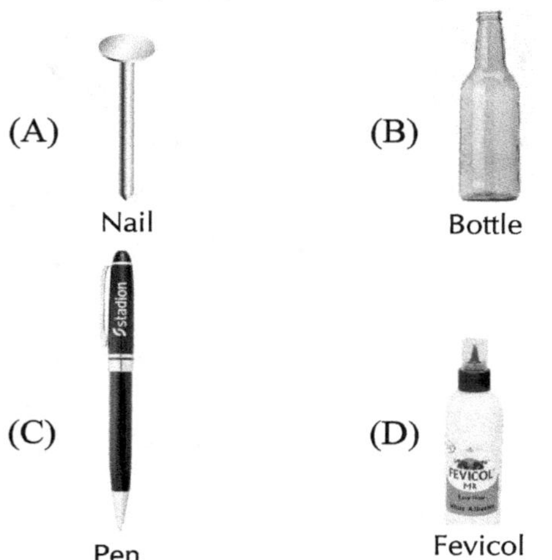

(C)

Pen

(D)

Fevicol

Direction (11–12) : Look at different strings.

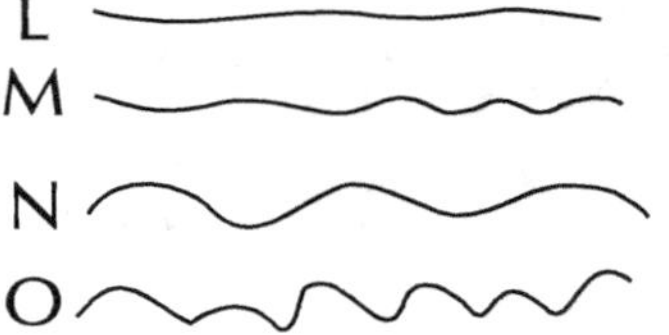

11. Which string is the longest?
(A) L   (B) M
(C) N   (D) O

12. Which string is the shortest?
(A) L   (B) M
(C) N   (D) O

13. Which penguin is nearest to the finish line?

(A) L   (B) M
(C) N   (D) O

14. Tape is __________ span long.

(A) 20   (B) 12
(C) 13   (D) 14

15. The girl is how many units tall?

(A) 12 units
(B) 10 units
(C) 14 units
(D) 16 units

16. Which tree is taller than the one given below?

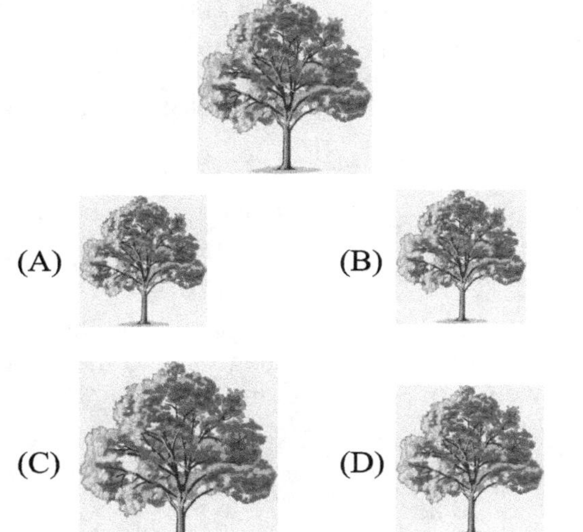

(A)   (B)

(C)   (D)

17. Which of the following has the least capacity?

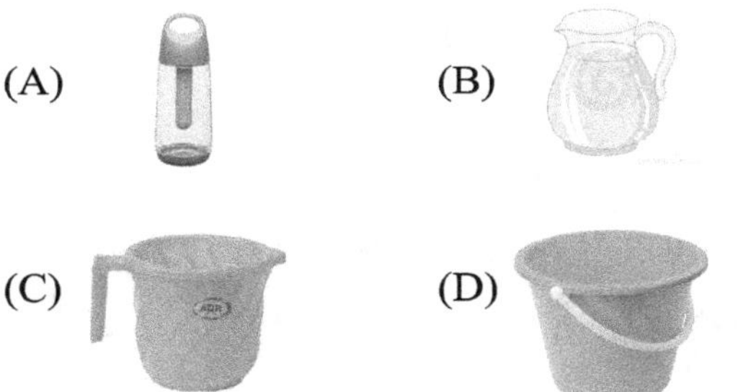

(A)   (B)

(C)   (D)

18. Which skeleton is shorter than C?

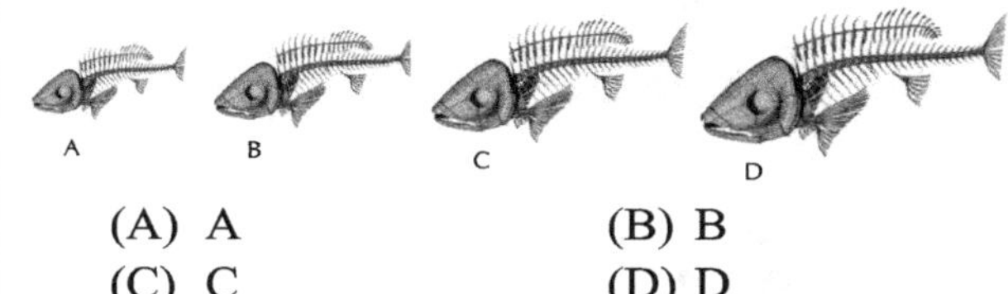

(A) A   (B) B
(C) C   (D) D

19. Which tree is the tallest?

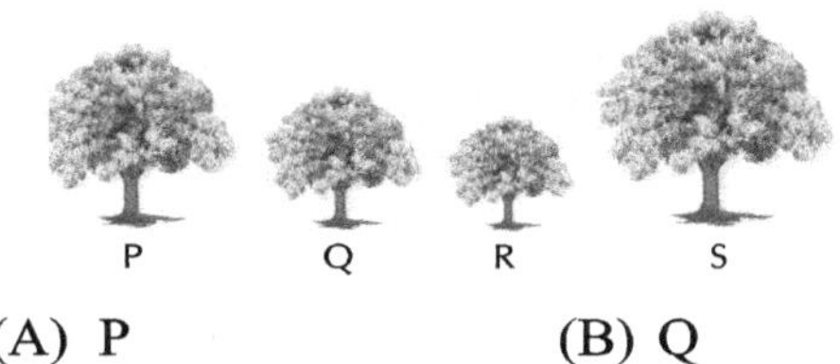

(A) P   (B) Q
(C) R   (D) S

20. Whose balloon has the shortest string?

(A) L
(B) M
(C) N
(D) O

HOTS (ACHIEVERS SECTION)

21. Measure the length of the ribbon to the nearest centimetres.

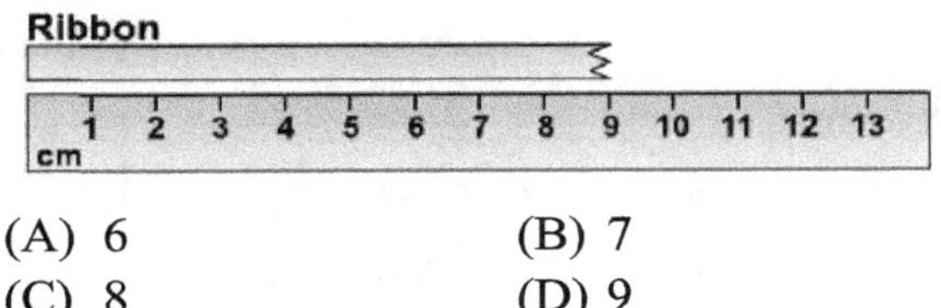

(A) 6   (B) 7
(C) 8   (D) 9

22. Which of the following would you use to hold water?

(A)

(B)

(C) 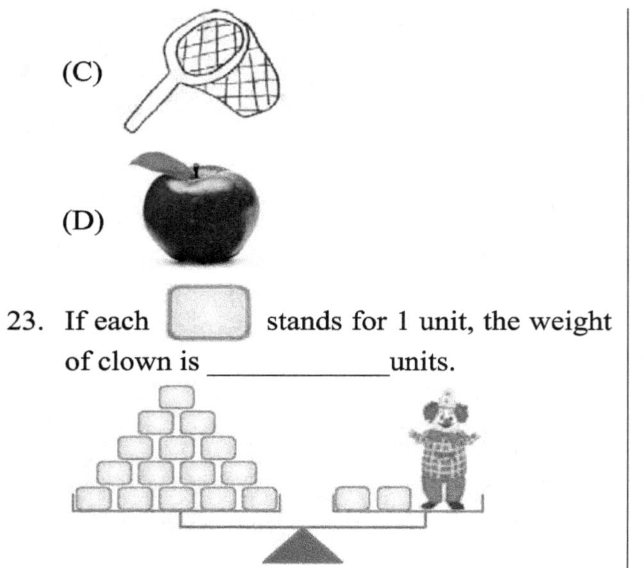

(D)

23. If each ☐ stands for 1 unit, the weight of clown is ____________ units.

(A) 15 units   (B) 13 units
(C) 12 units   (D) 11 units

24. Look at the boxes carefully.

100kg	50kg	80kg	200kg
A	B	C	D

Box ____________ is heavier than box A.
(A) A   (B) B
(C) C   (D) D

25. If weight of Sonu is 30 kg and weight of Arun is more than Sonu, then what is the possible weight of Arun from the following.
(A) 25 kg
(B) 40 kg
(C) 20 kg
(D) 29 kg

1.	A B C D	6.	A B C D	11.	A B C D	16	A B C D	21.	A B C D
2.	A B C D	7.	A B C D	12.	A B C D	17.	A B C D	22.	A B C D
3.	A B C D	8.	A B C D	13.	A B C D	18.	A B C D	23.	A B C D
4.	A B C D	9.	A B C D	14.	A B C D	19.	A B C D	24.	A B C D
5.	A B C D	10.	A B C D	15.	A B C D	20.	A B C D	25.	A B C D

OLYMPIAD WORKBOOK (IMO) CLASS– 1

TIME 

LEARNING OBJECTIVES

➤ Time

➤ Calendar

MULTIPLE CHOICE QUESTIONS

1. What do you do in the evening?
   (A) Play   (B) Sleep
   (C) Go to school   (D) Eating

2. When do you wake up?
   (A) Afternoon
   (B) Night
   (C) Morning
   (D) Evening

3. When do you have your breakfast?
   (A)    (B) 

   (C)   (D)

4. What do you do at night?
   (A) Sleep
   (B) Play
   (C) Go to school
   (D) Wash clothes

5. Suppose the sun is just above your head. What time of the day is it?
   (A) Morning
   (B) Noon
   (C) Evening
   (D) Night

6. Which of the following clocks shows 7'O clock?
   (A)   (B)

   (C)   (D)

7. Which of the following clocks shows time less than 5'O clock?
   (A) 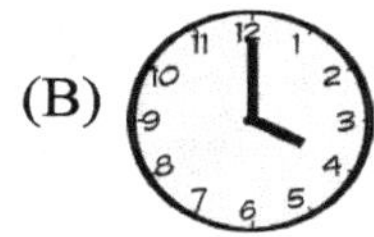   (B) 

   (C)    (D) 

8. Which of the following clocks shows time more than 6'O clock?
   (A) 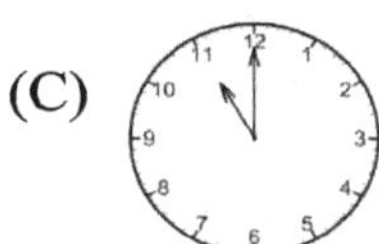   (B) 

   (C)    (D) 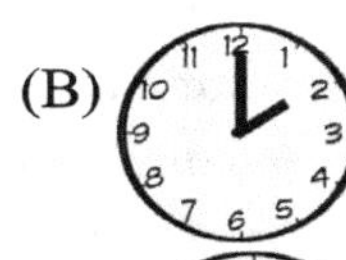

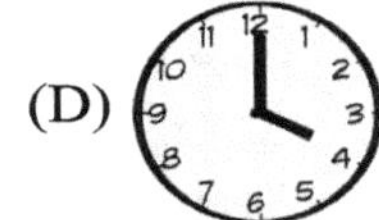

9. Which of these has second hand in the clock?

(A) 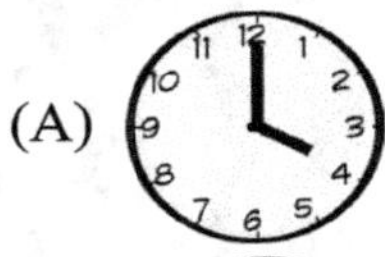

(B) 

(C) 

(D) 

10. Which of the following clocks shows time as 11'O clock?

(A) 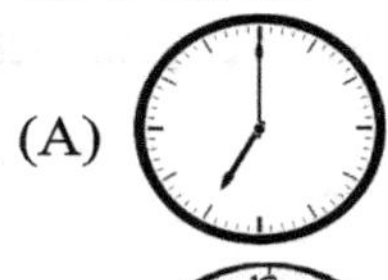

(B) 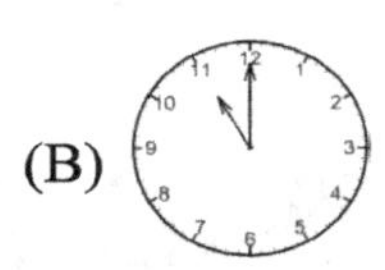

(C) 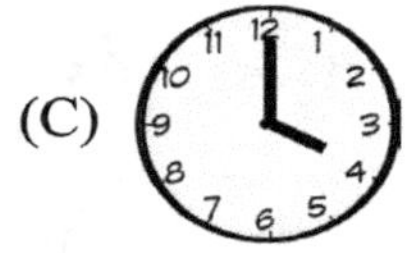

(D) 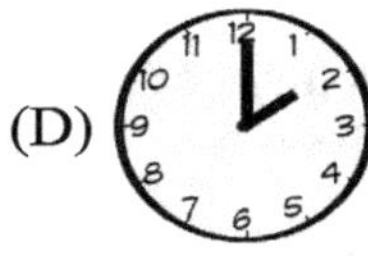

11. If today is Sunday, then tomorrow is ____________.

(A) Monday   (B) Saturday
(C) Tuesday   (D) Friday

12. If yesterday was Thursday, then today is ____________.

(A) Friday   (B) Wednesday
(C) Saturday   (D) Sunday

13. ____________ come after July and before November.

(A) January
(B) December
(C) June
(D) September

14. Which day comes just after Monday?
(A) Sunday
(B) Thursday
(C) Wednesday
(D) Tuesday

15. You play with your friends in playground in ____________.

(A) Evening   (B) Night
(C) Morning   (D) Day

16. Which activity you do at night?

(A)  Sleeping

(B) 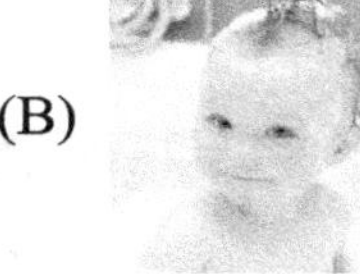 Bathing

(C)  Playing

(D) 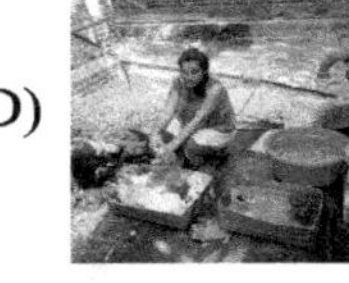 Washing

17. We wake up to go to school in
(A) Evening   (B) Night
(C) Morning   (D) Day

18. Which activity you do in morning?

(A)  Bathing

(B)  Playing

(C)  Dinner

(D) 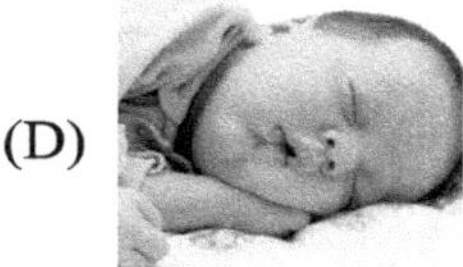 Sleeping

19. We go to bed at_________.
    (A) Day   (B) Night
    (C) Afternoon   (D) Morning
20. Where should be the hour hand and minute hand if it is 6'o clock?

(A) The hour hand on 6 and minute hand on 10
(B) The hour hand on 6 and minute hand on 6
(C) The hour hand on 6 and minute hand on 12
(D) Hour hand on 6 and minute hand on 1

HOTS (ACHIEVERS SECTION)

21. Which date is the third Saturday of July 20XX?

July 20XX						
S	M	T	W	T	F	S
					1	2
3	4	5	6	7	8	9
10	11	12	13	14	15	16
17	18	19	20	21	22	23
24	25	26	27	28	29	30
31						

    (A) July 10   (B) July 16
    (C) July 23   (D) July 30

22. How many days are there in 3 weeks?
    (A) 14 days   (B) 7 days
    (C) 13 days   (D) 21 days

23. How many months of a year has 31 days?
    (A) 7   (B) 6
    (C) 5   (D) 8

24. What is the 8th month of the year?

    (A) July   (B) October
    (C) August   (D) September

25. Which of the following months comes just before the ninth month of a year?
    (A) August   (B) September
    (C) October   (D) July

1.	Ⓐ Ⓑ Ⓒ Ⓓ	6.	Ⓐ Ⓑ Ⓒ Ⓓ	11.	Ⓐ Ⓑ Ⓒ Ⓓ	16	Ⓐ Ⓑ Ⓒ Ⓓ	21.	Ⓐ Ⓑ Ⓒ Ⓓ
2.	Ⓐ Ⓑ Ⓒ Ⓓ	7.	Ⓐ Ⓑ Ⓒ Ⓓ	12.	Ⓐ Ⓑ Ⓒ Ⓓ	17.	Ⓐ Ⓑ Ⓒ Ⓓ	22.	Ⓐ Ⓑ Ⓒ Ⓓ
3.	Ⓐ Ⓑ Ⓒ Ⓓ	8.	Ⓐ Ⓑ Ⓒ Ⓓ	13.	Ⓐ Ⓑ Ⓒ Ⓓ	18.	Ⓐ Ⓑ Ⓒ Ⓓ	23.	Ⓐ Ⓑ Ⓒ Ⓓ
4.	Ⓐ Ⓑ Ⓒ Ⓓ	9.	Ⓐ Ⓑ Ⓒ Ⓓ	14.	Ⓐ Ⓑ Ⓒ Ⓓ	19.	Ⓐ Ⓑ Ⓒ Ⓓ	24.	Ⓐ Ⓑ Ⓒ Ⓓ
5.	Ⓐ Ⓑ Ⓒ Ⓓ	10.	Ⓐ Ⓑ Ⓒ Ⓓ	15.	Ⓐ Ⓑ Ⓒ Ⓓ	20.	Ⓐ Ⓑ Ⓒ Ⓓ	25.	Ⓐ Ⓑ Ⓒ Ⓓ

MONEY

6

➤ Key Points on Money

MULTIPLE CHOICE QUESTIONS

1. Which has maximum cost?

(A)  ₹ 55

(B) 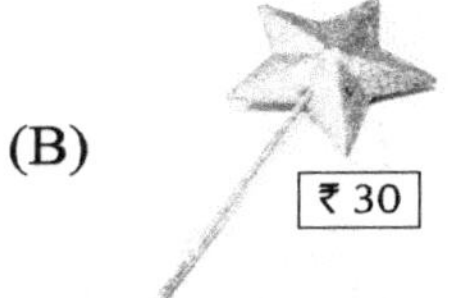 ₹ 30

(C) 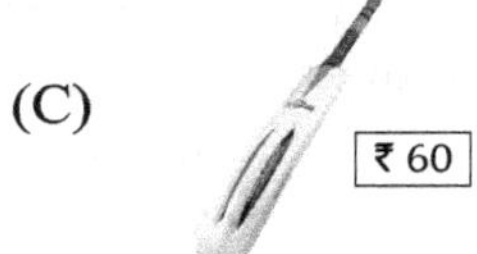 ₹ 60

(D)  ₹45

2. Which has minimum cost?

(A)  ₹ 100

(B)  ₹ 150

(C) 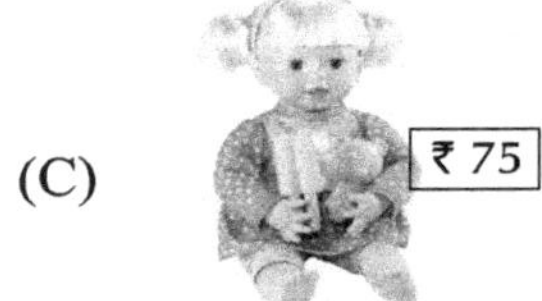 ₹ 75

(D) 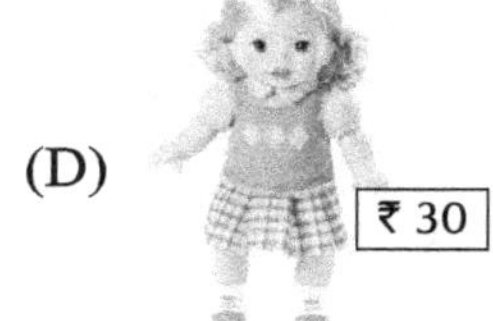 ₹ 30

3. Which amount is more than ₹ 100?
   (A) ₹ 20 (B) ₹ 100
   (C) ₹ 500 (D) ₹ 50 + ₹ 25

4. Ajay wants to exchange his ₹ 10 with some coins. Which set of coins he can take?

(A)  

(B) 

(C) 

(D) 

5.  ₹ 2 can be taken for __________.

(A) 

(B) 

(C) 

(D) 

6. How much money is enough to buy this doll?

(A) ₹ 10

(B) ₹ 30

(C) ₹ 100

(D) ₹ 25

7. Sonam has ₹ 100. Which of the following she can buy?

(A)  ₹ 125

(B) 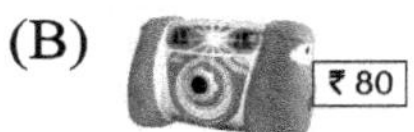 ₹ 80

(C)  ₹150

(D)  + ₹ 120

8. ₹ 30 = __________.

(A) Four ₹ 5 coins

(B) Two ₹ 10 coins

(C) Three ₹ 10 coins

(D) Three ₹ 5 coins

9. How much amount is shown?

(A) ₹ 10   (B) ₹ 12

(C) ₹ 7   (D) ₹ 15

10. How much amount is shown?

(A) ₹ 155   (B) ₹ 150

(C) ₹ 160   (D) ₹ 170

11. How much money is shown?

(A) ₹ 20   (B) ₹ 22

(C) ₹ 30   (D) ₹ 35

12. Which set of coins shows ₹ 4?

(A) 

(B) 

(C) 

(D) 

13. ₹ 6 = ?

(A) 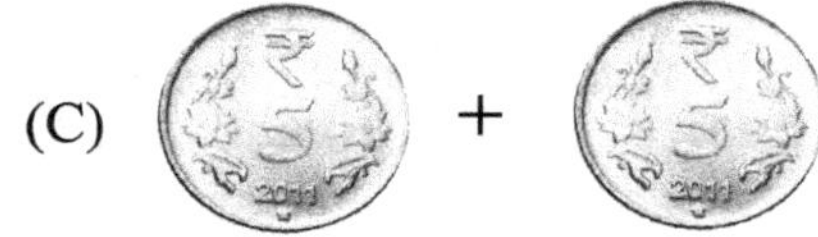

(B) 

(C) 

(D) 

14. How much amount is shown here?

(A) ₹ 20   (B) ₹ 50
(C) ₹ 2   (D) ₹ 25

15. How much amount is shown here?

(A) ₹ 72   (B) ₹ 60
(C) ₹ 12   (D) ₹ 50

16. Deepak gave ₹ 50 to buy this toy. How much will he get back?
(A) ₹ 10   (B) ₹ 20
(C) ₹ 35   (D) ₹ 30

17. Radha wants to buy 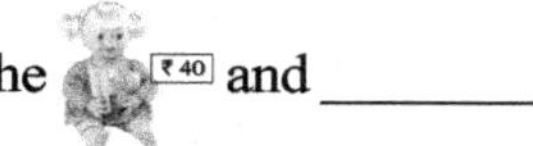 . She has ₹ 10. How much more does she need?
(A) ₹ 20   (B) ₹ 15
(C) ₹ 5   (D) ₹ 10

18. ₹10 + ₹10 + ₹10 = __________.
(A) ₹ 35   (B) ₹ 30
(C) ₹ 40   (D) ₹ 20

19. One doll costs ₹ 10. How much money does Priya need to pay for two dolls.
(A) 20   (B) 30
(C) 40   (D) 50

20. Shivam pays ₹ 70 for the ₹40 and __________.

(A)  ₹ 30

(B)  ₹ 20

(C)  ₹ 50

(D)  ₹ 50

21. If one pencil costs ₹10. How many pencils Riya can buy for ₹20.
    (A) 1
    (B) 2
    (C) 3
    (D) 4

22. Tanu has ₹50. She buy 2 pens and 1 pencil. Each pen cost ₹10 and cost of a pencil is ₹5. How much money is left with her now?
    (A) 30
    (B) 25
    (C) 35
    (D) 40

23. Which statement is incorrect.
    (A) ₹100 is more than ₹50
    (B) ₹50 + ₹250 = ₹300
    (C) ₹200 is twice of ₹100
    (D) ₹70 is less than ₹50

24. ₹100 − ₹ _________ = ₹60
    (A) ₹60
    (B) ₹40
    (C) ₹30
    (D) ₹50

25. Rohan has ₹100. How many cars he can buy from this money.

₹25

    (A) 3
    (B) 4
    (C) 2
    (D) 1

Darken Your Choice with HB Pencil

1.	Ⓐ Ⓑ Ⓒ Ⓓ	6.	Ⓐ Ⓑ Ⓒ Ⓓ	11.	Ⓐ Ⓑ Ⓒ Ⓓ	16	Ⓐ Ⓑ Ⓒ Ⓓ	21.	Ⓐ Ⓑ Ⓒ Ⓓ
2.	Ⓐ Ⓑ Ⓒ Ⓓ	7.	Ⓐ Ⓑ Ⓒ Ⓓ	12.	Ⓐ Ⓑ Ⓒ Ⓓ	17.	Ⓐ Ⓑ Ⓒ Ⓓ	22.	Ⓐ Ⓑ Ⓒ Ⓓ
3.	Ⓐ Ⓑ Ⓒ Ⓓ	8.	Ⓐ Ⓑ Ⓒ Ⓓ	13.	Ⓐ Ⓑ Ⓒ Ⓓ	18.	Ⓐ Ⓑ Ⓒ Ⓓ	23.	Ⓐ Ⓑ Ⓒ Ⓓ
4.	Ⓐ Ⓑ Ⓒ Ⓓ	9.	Ⓐ Ⓑ Ⓒ Ⓓ	14.	Ⓐ Ⓑ Ⓒ Ⓓ	19.	Ⓐ Ⓑ Ⓒ Ⓓ	24.	Ⓐ Ⓑ Ⓒ Ⓓ
5.	Ⓐ Ⓑ Ⓒ Ⓓ	10.	Ⓐ Ⓑ Ⓒ Ⓓ	15.	Ⓐ Ⓑ Ⓒ Ⓓ	20.	Ⓐ Ⓑ Ⓒ Ⓓ	25.	Ⓐ Ⓑ Ⓒ Ⓓ

GEOMETRICAL SHAPES

LEARNING OBJECTIVES

➤ Plane Shapes   ➤ Solid Shapes

MULTIPLE CHOICE QUESTIONS

1. Which object is on the chair?

(A)    (B) 

(C)    (D) 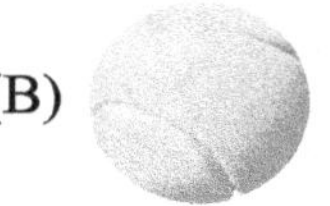

2. How many circles are there in the figure?

(A) 12   (B) 11
(C) 14   (D) 15

3. Which objects are outside the box?

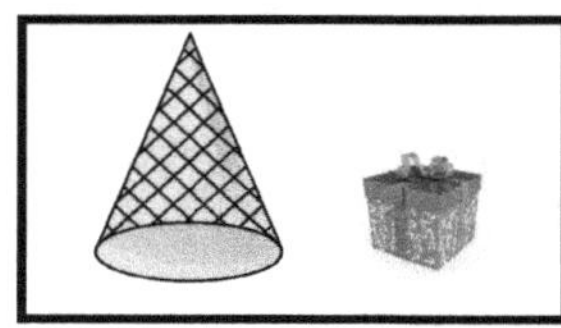 

(A) 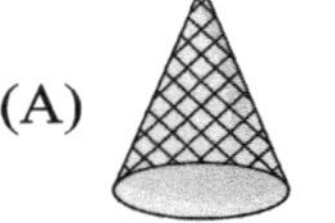

(B) 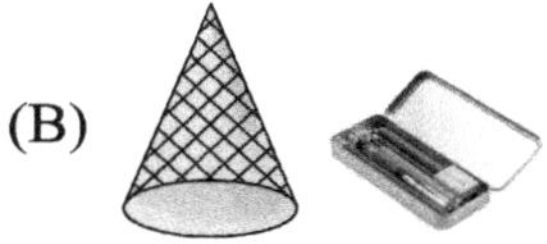

(C) 

(D) 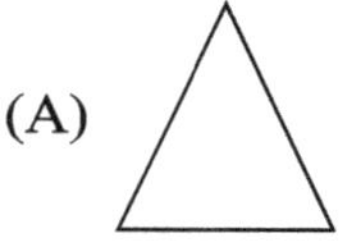

4. Which shape is a triangle?

(A) 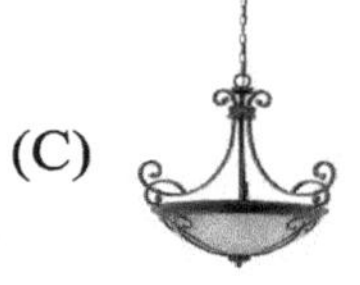

(B) 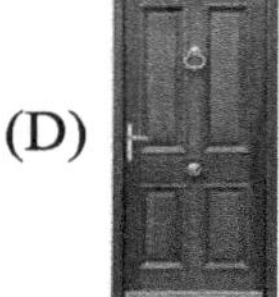

(C) 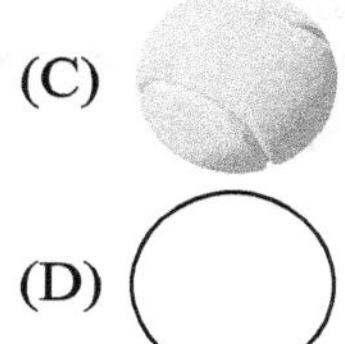

(D) 

5. Which of the following looks like a cube?

(A) 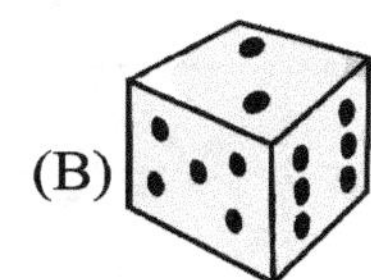

(B) 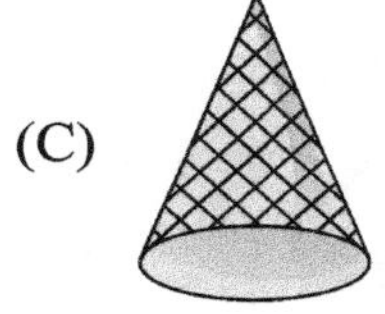

(C) 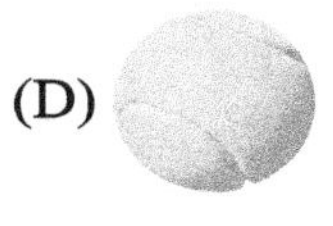

(D) 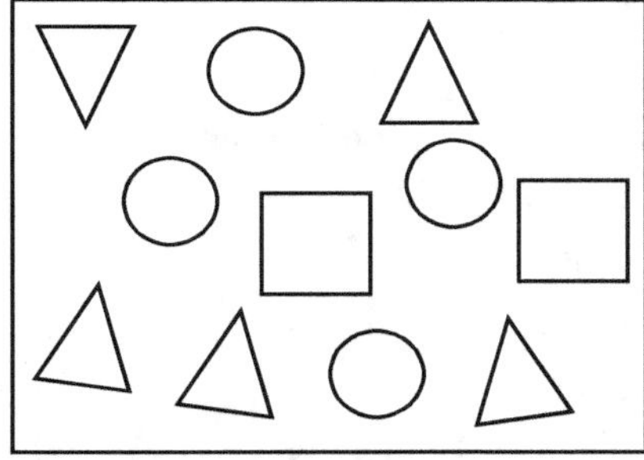

6. How many circles are there in the box?

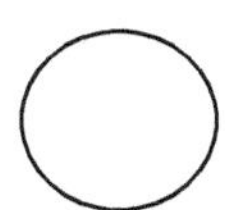

(A) 6   (B) 5
(C) 7   (D) 4

7. Name the shape which is shaded below.

(A) Triangle   (B) Square
(C) Rectangle   (D) Circle

8.  Name the shape of the shaded part ………… .

(A) Rectangle   (B) Triangle
(C) Circle   (D) Square

9. How many circles are there inside the big circle?

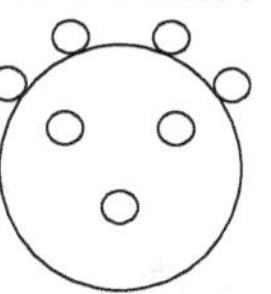

(A) 4   (B) 3
(C) 5   (D) 2

10. There are ………… more circles (○) in the clown's cap than the face.

(A) 2   (B) 3
(C) 1   (D) 0

11. Arrange the given balls from the biggest to the smallest?

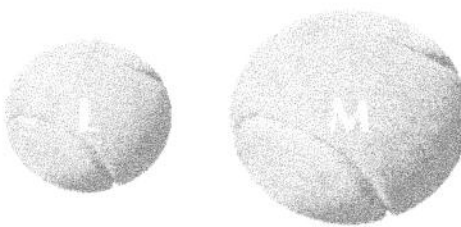

(A) L, M, N, O   (B) M, N, L, O
(C) O, L, N, M   (D) M, N, O, L

12. Select the correct match of the shapes that can be drawn, using given solid objects along these.

(A) 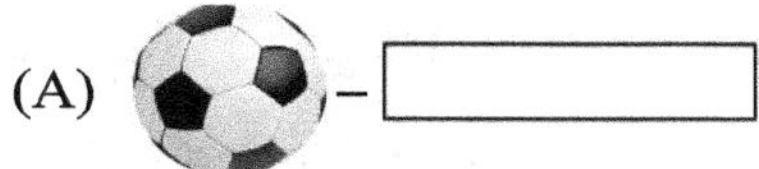 –

(B) 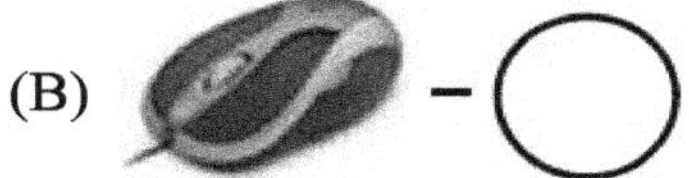 –

(C) 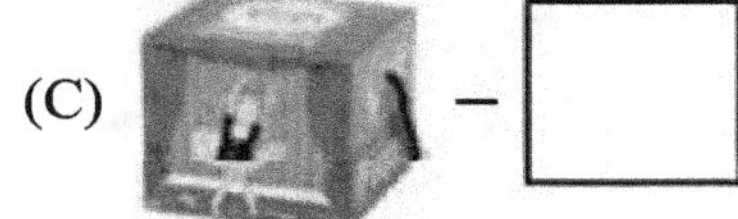 –

(D)  –

13. In which of the following group(s) the shape 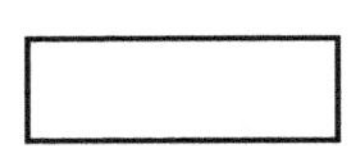 can be placed?

Group L 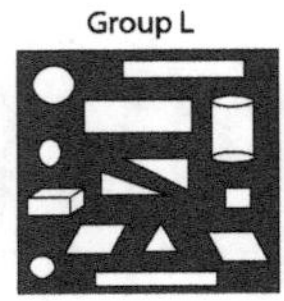 Group M 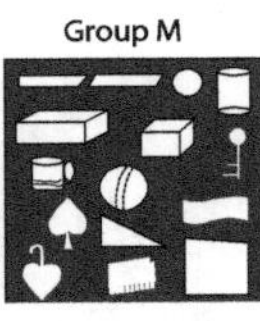 Group N 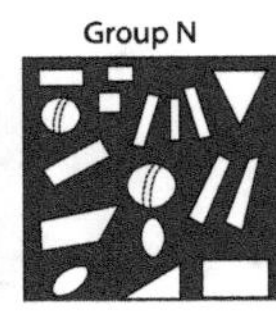 Group O 

(A) Both L and M
(B) Only L
(C) Only M
(D) L, M, N and O

14. Which figure is not shown below?

(A) Rectangle   (B) Triangle
(C) Square   (D) Circle

15. Count the total number of triangles.

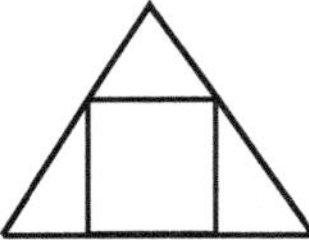

(A) 3   (B) 4
(C) 2   (D) 1

16. Amit has 4 groups of shapes.

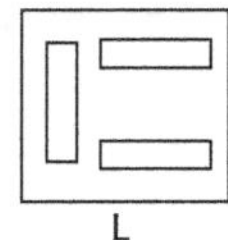   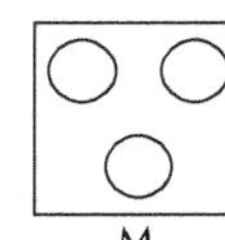   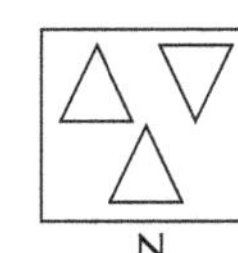   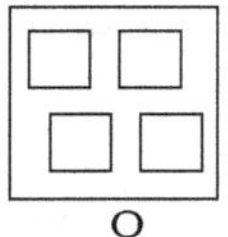
L   M   N   O

In which group he will put a ring?
(A) L   (B) M
(C) N   (D) O

17. What is the shape of a slice of the pizza?

(A) Rectangle   (B) Triangle
(C) Square   (D) Circle

18. Tanu draws a figure which consists of three triangles and one circle. Which of the following could be Tanu's drawing?

(A) 

(B) 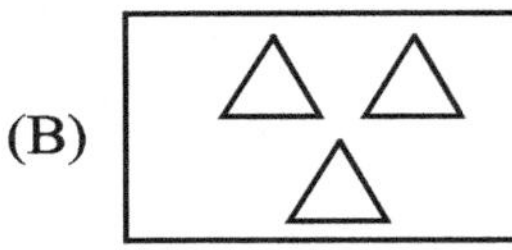

(C) 

(D) 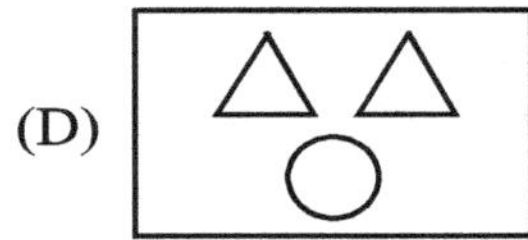

19. What is the shape of a dice?
(A) Cylinder
(B) Cube
(C) Cone
(D) Sphere

20. The rocket below is a combination of a __________ and a ________.

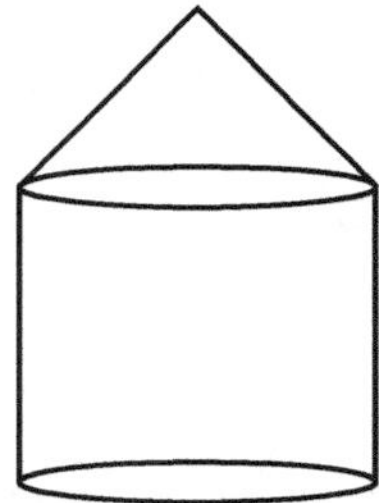

(A) Cuboid, Sphere
(B) Cone, Cube
(C) Cube, Cylinder
(D) Cone, Cylinder

21. Identify the object which is under the table and rolling also.

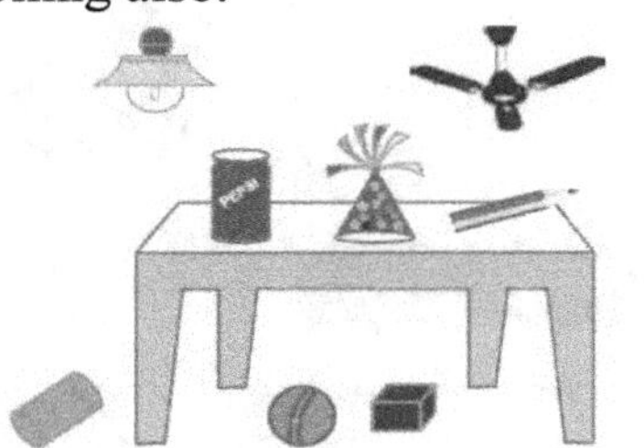

(A) 

(B) 

(C) 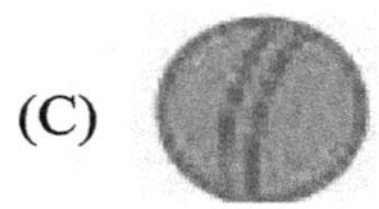

(D) 

22. Count the total number of squares.

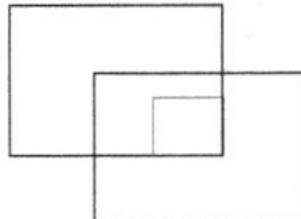

(A) 2

(B) 3

(C) 1

(D) 4

23. How many different types of shapes are there in the given figure?

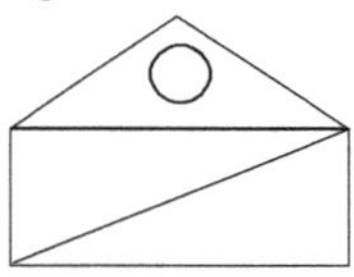

(A) 3

(B) 2

(C) 1

(D) 4

24. What is the shape of the surfaces of a cuboid?

(A) Circle

(B) Rectangle

(C) Triangle

(D) Oval

25. Match the following :

Shape	Numbers of sides
(A) Square	(i) 12
(B) Circle	(ii) 4
(C) Triangle	(iii) 0
(D) Cube	(iv) 3

(A) (A)→(ii); (B) →(iii); (C) →(iv); (D) →(i)

(B) (A) →(iii); (B) →(ii); (C) →(i); (D) →(iv)

(C) (A)→(ii); (B)→(i); (C)→(iii); (D)→(iv)

(D) (A) →(i); (B)→(ii); (C)→(iii); (D)→(iv)

Darken Your Choice with HB Pencil

1.	Ⓐ Ⓑ Ⓒ Ⓓ	6.	Ⓐ Ⓑ Ⓒ Ⓓ	11.	Ⓐ Ⓑ Ⓒ Ⓓ	16	Ⓐ Ⓑ Ⓒ Ⓓ	21.	Ⓐ Ⓑ Ⓒ Ⓓ
2.	Ⓐ Ⓑ Ⓒ Ⓓ	7.	Ⓐ Ⓑ Ⓒ Ⓓ	12.	Ⓐ Ⓑ Ⓒ Ⓓ	17.	Ⓐ Ⓑ Ⓒ Ⓓ	22.	Ⓐ Ⓑ Ⓒ Ⓓ
3.	Ⓐ Ⓑ Ⓒ Ⓓ	8.	Ⓐ Ⓑ Ⓒ Ⓓ	13.	Ⓐ Ⓑ Ⓒ Ⓓ	18.	Ⓐ Ⓑ Ⓒ Ⓓ	23.	Ⓐ Ⓑ Ⓒ Ⓓ
4.	Ⓐ Ⓑ Ⓒ Ⓓ	9.	Ⓐ Ⓑ Ⓒ Ⓓ	14.	Ⓐ Ⓑ Ⓒ Ⓓ	19.	Ⓐ Ⓑ Ⓒ Ⓓ	24.	Ⓐ Ⓑ Ⓒ Ⓓ
5.	Ⓐ Ⓑ Ⓒ Ⓓ	10.	Ⓐ Ⓑ Ⓒ Ⓓ	15.	Ⓐ Ⓑ Ⓒ Ⓓ	20.	Ⓐ Ⓑ Ⓒ Ⓓ	25.	Ⓐ Ⓑ Ⓒ Ⓓ

LOGICAL REASONING

LEARNING OBJECTIVES

- ➤ The concept of patterns
- ➤ Types of patterns
- ➤ Odd One Out (Classification)
- ➤ Steps to solve problems
- ➤ The concept of analogy
- ➤ Examples on analogy
- ➤ The concept of Ranking Test
- ➤ Types of Ranking Test
- ➤ Grouping of Figures
- ➤ Embedded Figures

MULTIPLE CHOICE QUESTIONS

1. Find the missing number in the given number pattern, if the series in both the patterns follows the same rule.

Pattern I	Pattern II
22	60
30	68
38	?

(A) 76   (B) 66
(C) 36   (D) 56

2. Find the missing number in the given number pattern.

80, 70, 55, 45, ?

(A) 25   (B) 30
(C) 20   (D) 35

3. Complete the pattern by choosing the next figure.

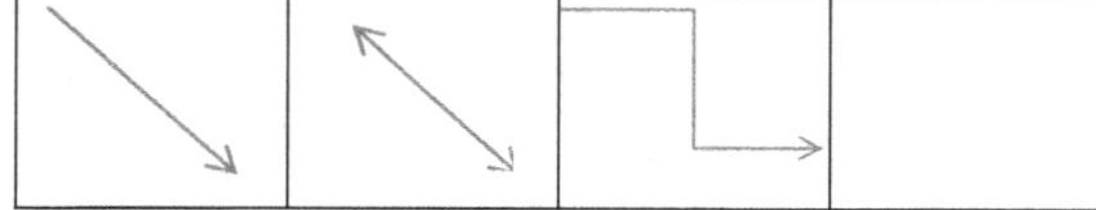

(A)   (B)

(C)   (D)

4. Complete the pattern by choosing the next figure.

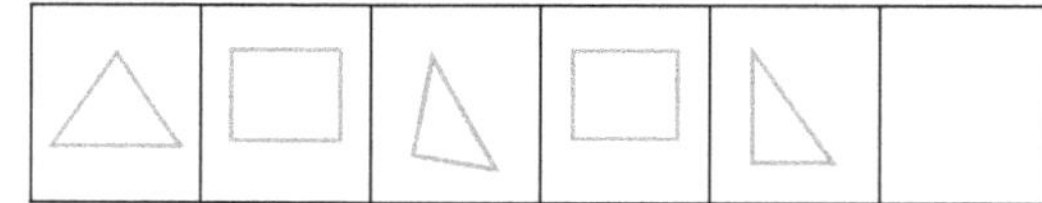

(A)   (B) 

(C)   (D) 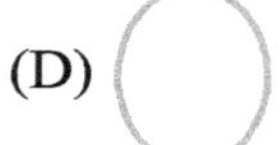

OLYMPIAD WORKBOOK (IMO) CLASS – 1

5. Complete the pattern by choosing the next figure.

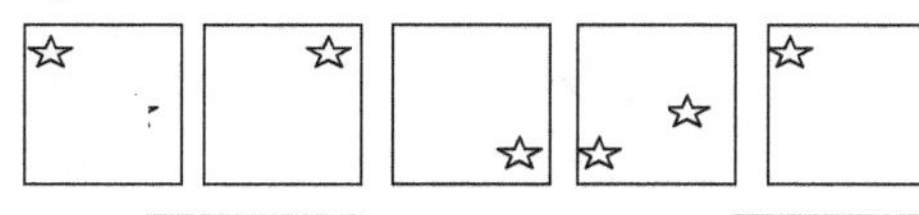

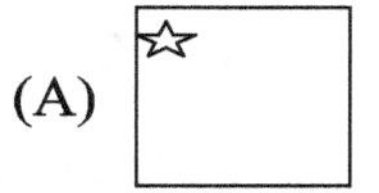

(A) 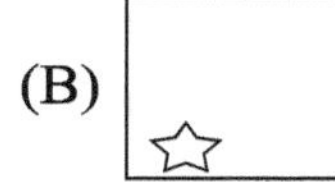

(B)

(C) 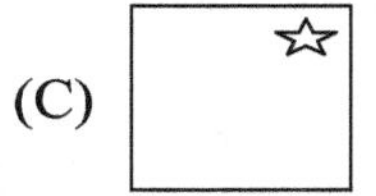

(D) 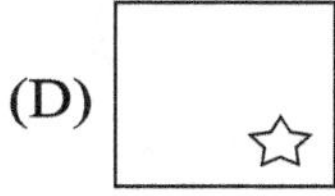

6. Find the odd one out.

(A) 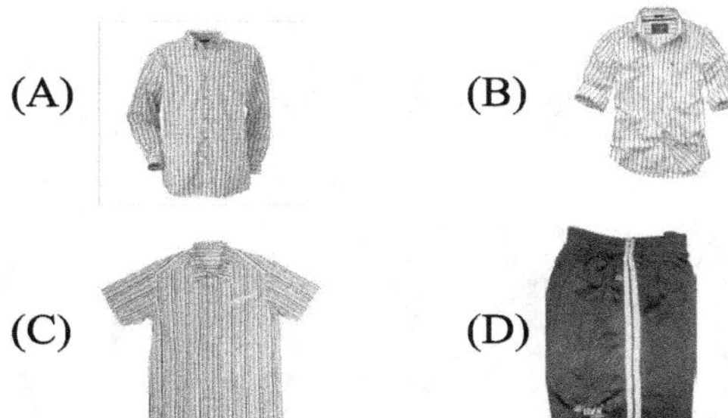

(B)

(C)

(D)

7. Find the odd one out.

(A) 

(B) 

(C) 

(D) 

8. Find the odd one out.

(A) 

(B) 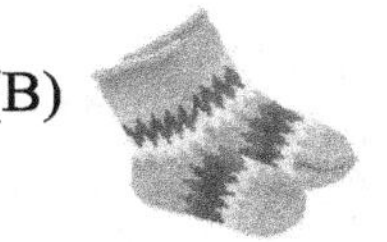

(C) 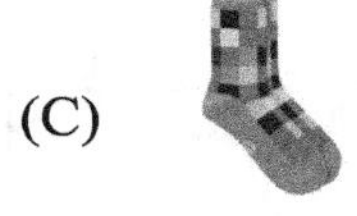

(D) 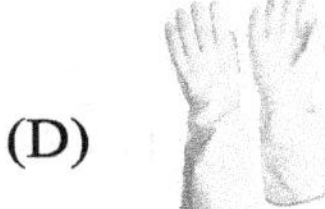

9. Find the odd one out.

(A) 

(B) 

(C) 

(D) 

10. Find the odd one out.
    (A) 2   (B) 4
    (C) 21   (D) A

11. Find out the relation.
    Month : 30 :: Week : ?
    (A) 10   (B) 7
    (C) 11   (D) 15

12. Find out the relation.
    Bread : Butter :: Tea : ?
    (A) Snacks   (B) Pizza
    (C) Coffee   (D) Milk

13. Find the missing shape by identifying the relationship.

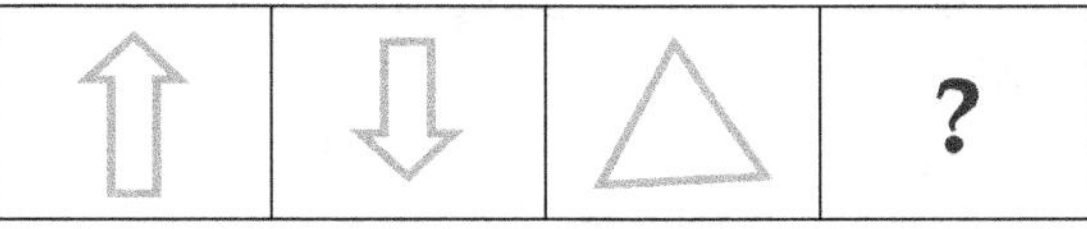

(A) 

(B) 

(C) 

(D) 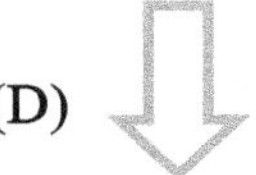

14. Find the missing shape by identifying the relationship.

(A) 

(B) 

(C) 

(D) 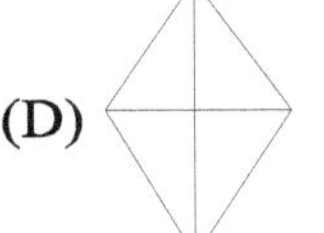

15. Find out the relation.

Father : Mother : : Grandfather : ?

(A) Grandson

(B) Daughter

(C) Grandmother

(D) Granddaughter

16. Which bird is seventh from the right end?

(A) M

(B) L

(C) N

(D) P

17. Bird O is second to the right of bird __________.

(A) P

(B) I

(C) M

(D) N

18. If bird P and I interchange their positions, then bird ________ is at the left end.

(A) I

(B) L

(C) P

(D) M

19. Bird J is just left to ______ bird.

(A) N

(B) O

(C) M

(D) L

20. Bird ____ is the sixth bird to the right of bird N.

(A) J

(B) K

(C) M

(D) L

21. How many groups of 3-stars are there?

(A) 24

(B) 3

(C) 8

(D) 10

22. How many groups of 2 rectangles can be formed from the group of assorted shapes given in the box?

(A) 1

(B) 2

(C) 4

(D) 3

23. Identify the group in which components can be divided into groups of four equally and completely.

A   B   C   D

24. How many groups of 2 giraffes are there?

(A) 10 (B) 9
(C) 18 (D) 20

25. How many groups of 4 bottles are there?

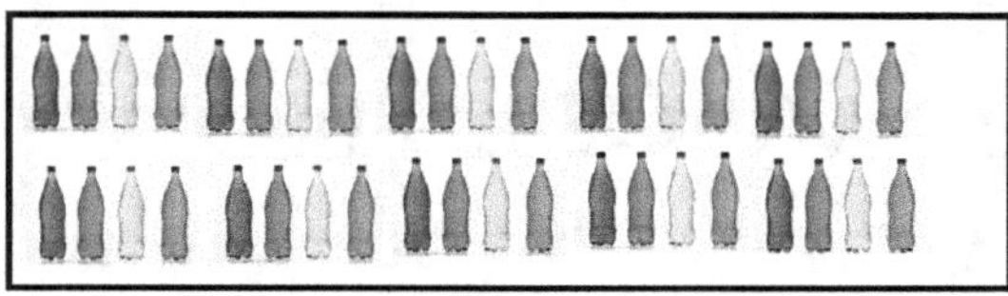

(A) 10 (B) 5
(C) 20 (D) 40

MODEL TEST PAPER

Section I : Logical Reasoning

1. How many different types of fruits are there in the basket?

(A) 4   (B) 5
(C) 7   (D) 6

2. If yesterday was Sunday , then tomorrow will be

Yesterday	Today	Tomorrow
Sunday	–	?

(A) Monday   (B) Tuesday
(C) Saturday   (D) Wednesday

3. Which smiley is 5th from the right end?

(A) T   (B) R
(C) Q   (D) U

4. Complete the given number pattern.

(A) 22   (B) 24
(C) 21   (D) 25

5. In the given image, the car is parked ————— the house.

(A) Inside   (B) Outside
(C) Above   (D) Below

6. Name the shape of the shaded face.

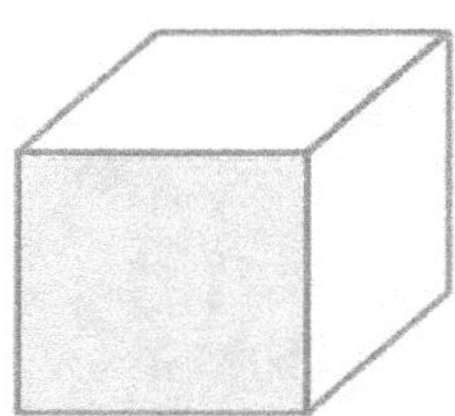

(A) Circle   (B) Square
(C) Oval   (D) Triangle

7. The given activity shows

(A) Morning   (B) Afternoon
(C) Evening   (D) Night

OLYMPIAD WORKBOOK (IMO) CLASS– 1

8. Select the figure which is as same as Figure (X).

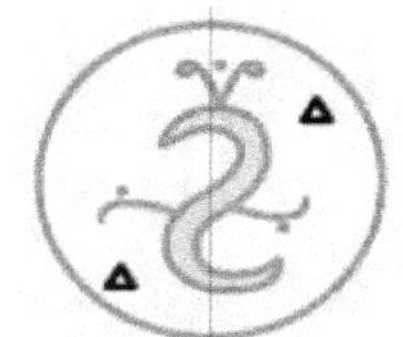

Figure (X)

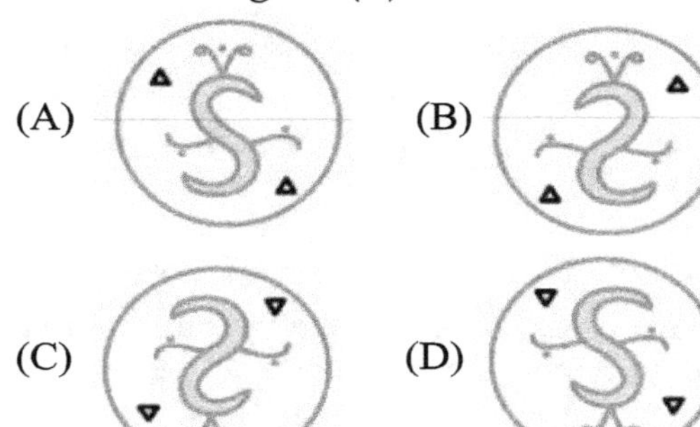

(A)   (B)   (C)   (D)

9. Which piece can be put together with shape P to make a square? Shape P

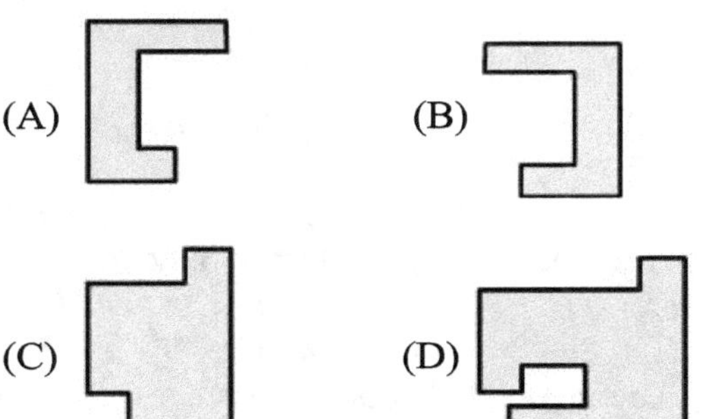

(A)   (B)   (C)   (D)

10. Rohit is taller than Samay but is shorter than Meeku. Who is the tallest?
    (A) Samay   (B) Meeku
    (C) Rohit   (D) None of these

Section II : Mathematical Reasoning

11. Which of the following options shows the largest number of pencils?

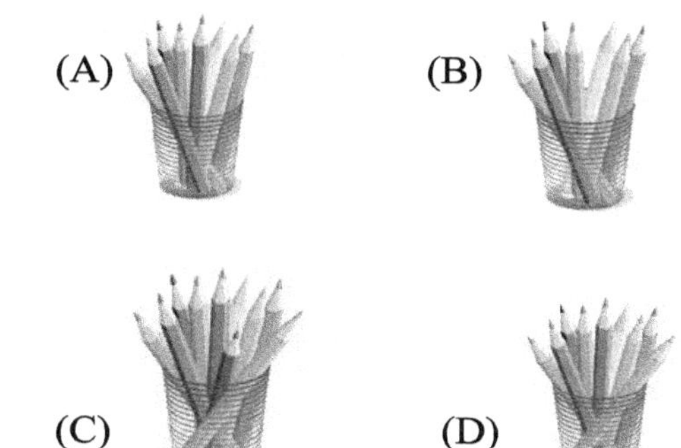

(A)   (B)   (C)   (D)

12. Which of the following subtraction is CORRECT?
    (A) $13 - 5 = 9$ (B) $19 - 4 = 15$
    (C) $17 - 7 = 12$ (D) $29 - 4 = 27$

13. If a rabbit starts jumping from 0, then it will finally reach at _______ in first Jump.

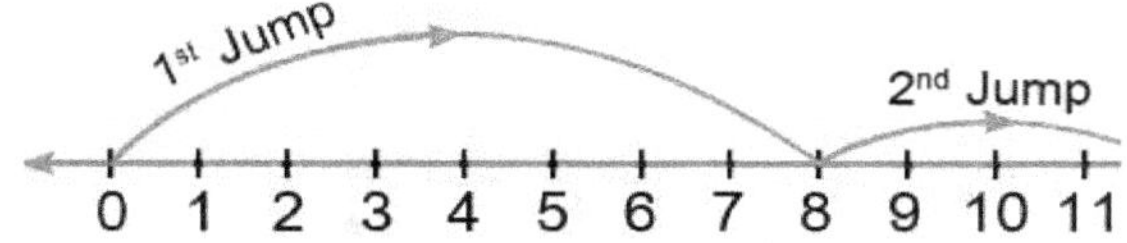

    (A) $0 + 8 = 8$ (B) $8 - 4 = 4$
    (C) $8 + 4 = 12$ (D) $12 + 8 = 20$

14. Which is the missing number in the number bond?

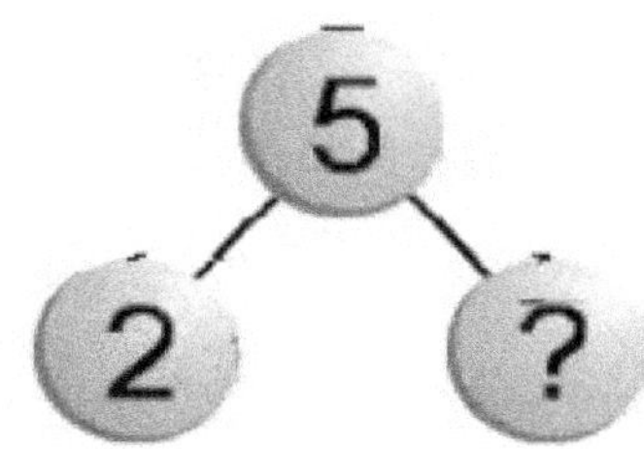

    (A) 1   (B) 2
    (C) 3   (D) 4

15. Elephant _________ is just before elephant A

    (A) C   (B) E
    (C) B   (D) D

16. The penguin is about _______  tall.

(A) 10   (B) 6
(C) 4   (D) 8

17. In which of the following options, numbers are arranged from the smallest to the greatest?
(A) 46, 25, 17, 3, 9   (B) 3, 9, 17, 25, 46
(C) 46, 25, 17, 9, 3   (D) 3, 9, 17, 46, 25

18. The number of straight lines in the given picture is

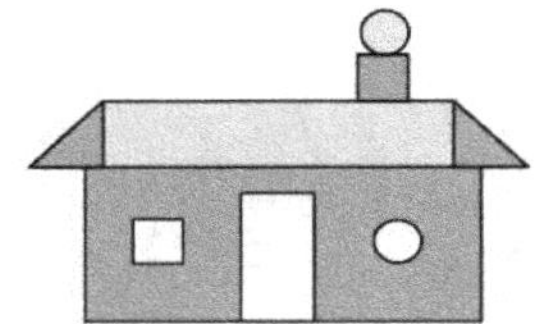

(A) 20   (B) 23
(C) 22   (D) 17

19. Find the number that is more than 5 + 6 but less than 10 + 3.
(A) 12   (B) 13
(C) 14   (D) 15

20. If '✡' means '−', then 8 ✡ 3 = ?

(A) 4   (B) 5
(C) 0   (D) 3

Section III : Everyday Mathematics

21. Anjali had 18 apples . She put 3 apples into each bag . She used _______ bags.

(A) 8   (B) 6
(C) 9   (D) 5

22. How much amount of money is shown here?

(A) ₹ 40   (B) ₹ 70
(C) ₹ 60   (D) ₹ 50

23. Priya baked 6 cakes. She baked 3 more cakes than Beena. Beena baked _____cakes.
(A) 2   (B) 4
(C) 3   (D) 6

24. Garima has 2 sticks A and B. Stick A is _______ units longer than stick B.

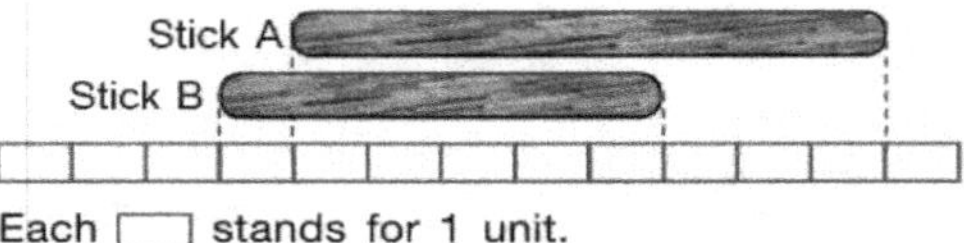

(A) 2   (B) 4
(C) 6   (D) 8

25. Anna had 17 balls. She gave away 6 balls. How many balls are left with her?
(A) 11   (B) 9
(C) 8   (D) 7

26. There are 12 horses. Three of them walk away. How many horses are left?

(A) 8   (B) 9
(C) 6   (D) 5

27. Mini has 14 toys and Riya has 5 toys. How many total toys both have?
(A) 15   (B) 19
(C) 9   (D) 20

28. Mohit needs to buy a chair and a lamp. How much does he need to pay?

(A) ₹ 15   (B) ₹ 70
(C) ₹ 22   (D) ₹ 45

29. Sarah had 16 toffees. If she put all the toffees in 4 boxes equally, then she has ________ toffees in each box.

(A) 2   (B) 4
(C) 6   (D) 8

30. Out of 9 books that Ruchi has, 3 are Mathematics books and the rest are English books. Ruchi has ________ English books.

(A) 4   (B) 7
(C) 8   (D) 6

Section IV : Achievers Section

31. 2 tens 7 ones – 1 tens 6 ones = ?

(A) 17   (B) 16
(C) 11   (D) 19

32. There are ________ more birds than cats.

(A) 3   (B) 8
(C) 4   (D) 9

33. The number of squares is ________ more than the number of triangles.

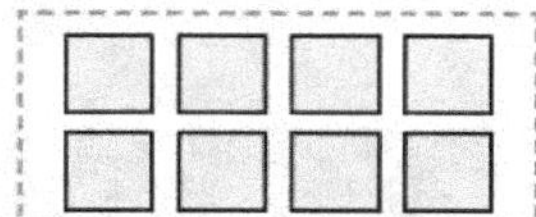
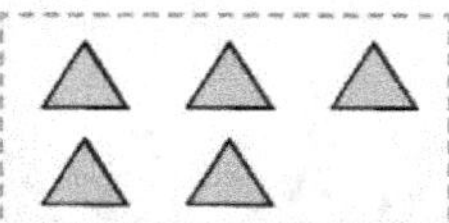

(A) 3 tens – 0 ones
(B) 2 tens
(C) 5 ones – 2 ones
(D) 8 ones + 2 ones

34. The missing number in the box is

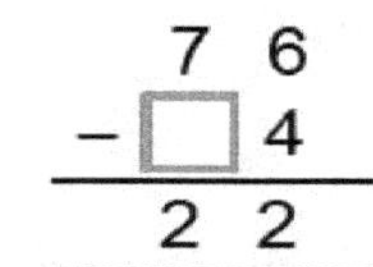

(A) 5   (B) 4
(C) 3   (D) 2

35. Which abacus shows 3 more than 61?

(A) 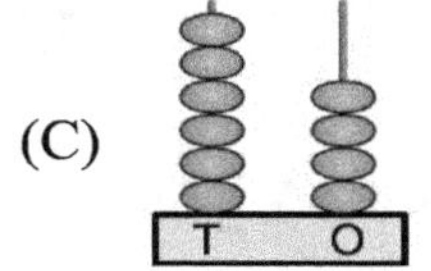   (B) 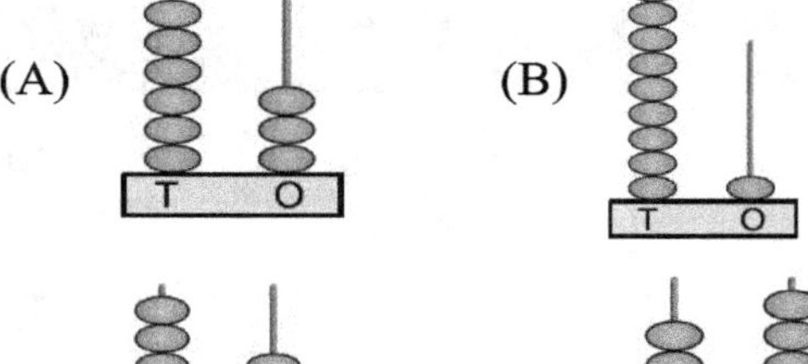

(C)   (D) 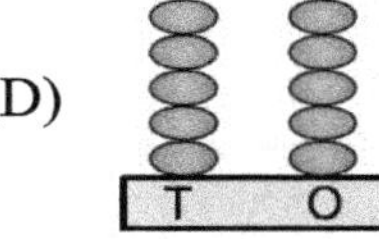

──────── Darken Your Choice with HB Pencil ────────

1.	Ⓐ Ⓑ Ⓒ Ⓓ	8.	Ⓐ Ⓑ Ⓒ Ⓓ	15.	Ⓐ Ⓑ Ⓒ Ⓓ	22	Ⓐ Ⓑ Ⓒ Ⓓ	29.	Ⓐ Ⓑ Ⓒ Ⓓ
2.	Ⓐ Ⓑ Ⓒ Ⓓ	9.	Ⓐ Ⓑ Ⓒ Ⓓ	16.	Ⓐ Ⓑ Ⓒ Ⓓ	23.	Ⓐ Ⓑ Ⓒ Ⓓ	30.	Ⓐ Ⓑ Ⓒ Ⓓ
3.	Ⓐ Ⓑ Ⓒ Ⓓ	10.	Ⓐ Ⓑ Ⓒ Ⓓ	17.	Ⓐ Ⓑ Ⓒ Ⓓ	24.	Ⓐ Ⓑ Ⓒ Ⓓ	31.	Ⓐ Ⓑ Ⓒ Ⓓ
4.	Ⓐ Ⓑ Ⓒ Ⓓ	11.	Ⓐ Ⓑ Ⓒ Ⓓ	18.	Ⓐ Ⓑ Ⓒ Ⓓ	25.	Ⓐ Ⓑ Ⓒ Ⓓ	32.	Ⓐ Ⓑ Ⓒ Ⓓ
5.	Ⓐ Ⓑ Ⓒ Ⓓ	12.	Ⓐ Ⓑ Ⓒ Ⓓ	19.	Ⓐ Ⓑ Ⓒ Ⓓ	26.	Ⓐ Ⓑ Ⓒ Ⓓ	33.	Ⓐ Ⓑ Ⓒ Ⓓ
6.	Ⓐ Ⓑ Ⓒ Ⓓ	13.	Ⓐ Ⓑ Ⓒ Ⓓ	20.	Ⓐ Ⓑ Ⓒ Ⓓ	27.	Ⓐ Ⓑ Ⓒ Ⓓ	34.	Ⓐ Ⓑ Ⓒ Ⓓ
7.	Ⓐ Ⓑ Ⓒ Ⓓ	14.	Ⓐ Ⓑ Ⓒ Ⓓ	21.	Ⓐ Ⓑ Ⓒ Ⓓ	28.	Ⓐ Ⓑ Ⓒ Ⓓ	35.	Ⓐ Ⓑ Ⓒ Ⓓ

HINTS AND SOLUTIONS

1. NUMBERS

Answer Key

1. (C)	2. (D)	3. (B)	4. (C)	5. (B)	6. (A)	7. (B)	8. (B)	9. (C)	10. (A)
11. (B)	12. (B)	13. (D)	14. (B)	15. (A)	16. (A)	17. (B)	18. (C)	19. (C)	20. (C)

4. (C)

5-Five is correct.

10. (A)

1 more than $4 = 5$ $(1 + 4)$

$\therefore$ (a) is correct answer.

14. (B)

Seventh is the ordinal number of 7.

15. (A)

Successor of $28 = 28 + 1 = 29$

18. (C)

Key is fourth from the left in the given set.

HOTS (ACHIEVERS SECTION)

21. (C)	22. (B)	23. (D)	24. (C)	25. (C)

2. ADDITION

Answer Key

1. (A)	2. (B)	3. (D)	4. (B)	5. (B)	6. (A)	7. (D)	8. (B)	9. (A)	10. (C)
11. (B)	12. (C)	13. (B)	14. (B)	15. (B)	16. (D)	17. (B)	18. (C)	19. (C)	20. (D)

1. (A)

Here we see

$$4 + 4 = 8$$

4. (B)

Here, $\quad 6 + 3 = 9, \qquad 6 + 4 = 10$

$\qquad 5 + 4 = 9, \qquad 4 + 4 = 8$

$\therefore$ (B) is incorrect.

11. (B)

Here, $5 + 5 = 10$

$\therefore$ Only (B) is correct.

12. (C)

We see, $\quad 50 + 6 = 56, \; 50 + 9 = 59$

$\qquad\qquad\qquad 60 + 12 = 72, \qquad 50 + 3 = 53$

$\therefore$ (C) is the biggest number.

16. (D)

Sum of the numbers of Shubhra's cards

$= 4 + 1 + 5 = 10$

17. (B)

Total stamps $= 35 + 43 = 78$

18. (C)

Shraddha's total marks $= 38 + 50 = 88$

20. (D)

Total no. of dolls $= 6 + 3 = 9$

HOTS (ACHIEVERS SECTION)

21. (B)	22. (C)	23. (C)	24. (C)	25. (A)

OLYMPIAD WORKBOOK (IMO) CLASS – 1

3. SUBTRACTION

Answer Key

1. (A)	2. (B)	3. (A)	4. (B)	5. (D)	6. (B)	7. (C)	8. (A)	9. (B)	10. (B)
11. (A)	12. (B)	13. (A)	14. (B)	15. (B)	16. (A)	17. (B)	18. (A)	19. (B)	20. (C)

1. **(A)**
    We have 4 tens 3 ones - 2 tens 2 ones
    $$= 4 \times 10 + 3 \times 1 - 2 \times 10 + 2 \times 1$$
    $$= 40 + 3 - 20 + 2$$
    $$= 43 - 22 = 21$$

3. **(A)**
    Here, $30 - 12 = 18$

4. **(B)**
    $13 - 3 = 10$
    and $11 - 5 = 6, \qquad 15 - 5 = 10$
    $\qquad 12 - 4 = 8, \qquad 9 - 3 = 6$
    $\therefore$ (B) is same as $13 - 3$.

8. **(A)**
    Here
    $\square - \square = 20 - 10 = 10$

10. **(B)**
    Required difference $= 98 - 16 = 82$

15. **(B)**
    We have $8 - 2 = 6$
    and $\qquad 12 - 2 = 10$
    $\qquad\qquad 12 - 6 = 6$
    $\therefore$ (b) is same as $8 - 2$.

17. **(B)**
    Remaining pages $= 55 - 40 = 15$

18. **(A)**
    Remaining sweets $= 99 - 46 = 53$

HOTS (ACHIEVERS SECTION)

21. (D)	22. (A)	23. (A)	24. (B)	25. (B)

4. LENGTHS, WEIGHTS & COMPARISONS

Answer Key

1. (A)	2. (D)	3. (A)	4. (A)	5. (B)	6. (D)	7. (A)	8. (D)	9. (B)	10. (A)
11. (D)	12. (A)	13. (D)	14. (A)	15. (C)	16. (C)	17. (A)	18. (A)	19. (D)	20. (C)

5. **(B)**
    Pencil is lightest.

6. **(D)**
    Pen is lighter than book.

8. **(D)**
    Spider S is farthest to the ladder.

10. **(A)**
    Nail is thinner than pen.

13. **(D)**
    Penguin O is nearest to the finish.

17. **(A)** Bottle has least capacity.

HOTS (ACHIEVERS SECTION)

21. (D)	22. (A)	23. (A)	24. (B)	25. (B)

21. **(D)**
    Length of ribbon $= 9$ cm

24. **(D)**
    Box D is heavier than box A

25. **(B)**
    Weight of Sonu $= 30$ kg
    Arun's weight is more than Sonu
    So, the possible weight of Arun is 40 kg

Answer Key

1. (A)	2. (C)	3. (B)	4. (A)	5. (B)	6. (C)	7. (D)	8. (C)	9. (D)	10. (B)
11. (A)	12. (A)	13. (D)	14. (D)	15. (A)	16. (A)	17. (C)	18. (A)	19. (B)	20. (C)

7. (D)
4 is less than 5.

8. (C)
11 is more than 6.

13. (D)
September comes after July and before November.

14. (D)
Tuesday comes after Monday.

HOTS (ACHIEVERS SECTION)

21. (B)	22. (D)	23. (A)	24. (C)	25. (A)

21. (B)
July 16 is third Saturday of July 20 xx

22. (D)
Number of days in one week = 7
Number of days in 3 weeks = 7+7+7= 21

23. (A)
7 months of a year have 31 days.

25. (A)
Ninth month of a year is September. The month that comes just before September is August.

6. MONEY

Answer Key

1. (C)	2. (D)	3. (C)	4. (D)	5. (A)	6. (B)	7. (B)	8. (C)	9. (A)	10. (B)
11. (B)	12. (B)	13. (A)	14. (D)	15. (B)	16. (C)	17. (C)	18. (B)	19. (A)	20. (A)

8. (C)
Six 50 paise coin = ₹ 3

15. (B)
Money = 50 + 10 = ₹ 60

16. (C)
Required money = 50 − 15 = ₹ 35

17. (C)
Radha needed = 15 − 10 = ₹ 5

18. (B)
Cost of 3 pens = 3 × 10 = ₹ 30

HOTS (ACHIEVERS SECTION)

21. (B)	22. (B)	23. (D)	24. (B)	25. (B)

21. (B)
Cost of 1 pencil = ₹ 10
Riya can buy (10 + 10) 2 pencils for ₹ 20

23. (D)
₹70 is less than ₹ 50 is incorrect

25. (B)
Rohan has ₹100
Price of one toy car = ₹ 25
He can buy = ₹ (25+25+25+25)
= 4 toy cars

7. GEOMETRICAL SHAPES

Answer Key

1. (B)	2. (C)	3. (C)	4. (A)	5. (B)	6. (D)	7. (B)	8. (A)	9. (B)	10. (A)
11. (B)	12. (C)	13. (D)	14. (C)	15. (B)	16. (B)	17. (B)	18. (C)	19. (B)	20. (D)

HOTS (ACHIEVERS SECTION)

21. (C)	22. (D)	23. (A)	24. (B)	25. (A)

21. (C) ⬤ is under the table and is rolling also.

22. (D) Total numbers of squares = 4

24. (B) Rectangle

8. LOGICAL REASONING

Answer Key

1. (A)	2. (B)	3. (B)	4. (C)	5. (B)	6. (D)	7. (D)	8. (C)	9. (C)	10. (D)
11. (B)	12. (A)	13. (A)	14. (D)	15. (C)	16. (C)	17. (B)	18. (A)	19. (C)	20. (D)
21. (C)	22. (D)	23. (A)	24. (B)	25. (A)					

1. (A)
Add 8 in each number.

2. (B)
Pattern followed in the given series is:
$80 - 10 = 70 \rightarrow 70 - 15 = 55 \rightarrow 55 - 10 = 45 \rightarrow 45 - 15 = 30$

4. (C)
Every second figure is a square.

13. (A)
First figure rotates vertically downwards.

14. (D)
Joining different parts to form a complete figure

15. (C)
As mother is opposite to father; similarly grandmother is opposite to grandfather.

MODEL TEST PAPER

Answer Key

1. (B)	2. (B)	3. (B)	4. (A)	5. (B)	6. (B)	7. (A)	8. (B)	9. (C)	10. (B)
11. (C)	12. (B)	13. (A)	14. (C)	15. (B)	16. (D)	17. (B)	18. (D)	19. (A)	20. (B)
21. (B)	22. (C)	23. (C)	24. (A)	25. (A)	26. (B)	27. (B)	28. (D)	29. (B)	30. (D)
31. (C)	32. (A)	33. (C)	34. (A)	35. (C)					

SAMPLE OMR ANSWER SHEET

1. STUDENT NAME (IN ENGLISH CAPITAL LETTERS ONLY)

Students must write and darken the respective circles completely using HB Pencil only. Othewise their Answer Sheets will not be evaluated.

PERSONAL DETAILS

2. SCHOOL CODE

3. CLASS

4. SECTION

5. ROLL NO.

6. QUESTION PAPER SET

A ○
B ○
C ○
D ○

7. MOBILE NUMBER

8. GENDER

MALE ○
FEMALE ○

9. STREAM
(Only for Class XI and XII Students)

MATHEMATICS ○
BIOLOGY ○
OTHERS ○

MARK YOUR ANSWERS

1.	Ⓐ Ⓑ Ⓒ Ⓓ	26.	Ⓐ Ⓑ Ⓒ Ⓓ
2.	Ⓐ Ⓑ Ⓒ Ⓓ	27.	Ⓐ Ⓑ Ⓒ Ⓓ
3.	Ⓐ Ⓑ Ⓒ Ⓓ	28.	Ⓐ Ⓑ Ⓒ Ⓓ
4.	Ⓐ Ⓑ Ⓒ Ⓓ	29.	Ⓐ Ⓑ Ⓒ Ⓓ
5.	Ⓐ Ⓑ Ⓒ Ⓓ	30.	Ⓐ Ⓑ Ⓒ Ⓓ
6.	Ⓐ Ⓑ Ⓒ Ⓓ	31.	Ⓐ Ⓑ Ⓒ Ⓓ
7.	Ⓐ Ⓑ Ⓒ Ⓓ	32.	Ⓐ Ⓑ Ⓒ Ⓓ
8.	Ⓐ Ⓑ Ⓒ Ⓓ	33.	Ⓐ Ⓑ Ⓒ Ⓓ
9.	Ⓐ Ⓑ Ⓒ Ⓓ	34.	Ⓐ Ⓑ Ⓒ Ⓓ
10.	Ⓐ Ⓑ Ⓒ Ⓓ	35.	Ⓐ Ⓑ Ⓒ Ⓓ
11.	Ⓐ Ⓑ Ⓒ Ⓓ	36.	Ⓐ Ⓑ Ⓒ Ⓓ
12.	Ⓐ Ⓑ Ⓒ Ⓓ	37.	Ⓐ Ⓑ Ⓒ Ⓓ
13.	Ⓐ Ⓑ Ⓒ Ⓓ	38.	Ⓐ Ⓑ Ⓒ Ⓓ
14.	Ⓐ Ⓑ Ⓒ Ⓓ	39.	Ⓐ Ⓑ Ⓒ Ⓓ
15.	Ⓐ Ⓑ Ⓒ Ⓓ	40.	Ⓐ Ⓑ Ⓒ Ⓓ
16.	Ⓐ Ⓑ Ⓒ Ⓓ	41.	Ⓐ Ⓑ Ⓒ Ⓓ
17.	Ⓐ Ⓑ Ⓒ Ⓓ	42.	Ⓐ Ⓑ Ⓒ Ⓓ
18.	Ⓐ Ⓑ Ⓒ Ⓓ	43.	Ⓐ Ⓑ Ⓒ Ⓓ
19.	Ⓐ Ⓑ Ⓒ Ⓓ	44.	Ⓐ Ⓑ Ⓒ Ⓓ
20.	Ⓐ Ⓑ Ⓒ Ⓓ	45.	Ⓐ Ⓑ Ⓒ Ⓓ
21.	Ⓐ Ⓑ Ⓒ Ⓓ	46.	Ⓐ Ⓑ Ⓒ Ⓓ
22.	Ⓐ Ⓑ Ⓒ Ⓓ	47.	Ⓐ Ⓑ Ⓒ Ⓓ
23.	Ⓐ Ⓑ Ⓒ Ⓓ	48.	Ⓐ Ⓑ Ⓒ Ⓓ
24.	Ⓐ Ⓑ Ⓒ Ⓓ	49.	Ⓐ Ⓑ Ⓒ Ⓓ
25.	Ⓐ Ⓑ Ⓒ Ⓓ	50.	Ⓐ Ⓑ Ⓒ Ⓓ

Signature of the Student & Date of Examination

Signature of the Invigilator & Date of Examination

V&S Publishers, F-2/16 Ansari Road, Daryaganj, New Delhi-110002, ☎ 011-23240026-27
✉ info@vspublishers.com, 🌐 www.vspublishers.com